Ibn ʿAbd al-Wahhab

TITLES IN THE MAKERS OF THE MUSLIM WORLD SERIES

Series Editor: Patricia Crone, Institute for Advanced Study, Princeton

Abd al-Ghani al-Nabulusi, Samer Akkach
'Abd al-Malik, Chase F. Robinson
Abd al-Rahman III, Maribel Fierro
Abu Nuwas, Philip Kennedy
Ahmad al-Mansur, Mercedes García-Arenal
Ahmad ibn Hanbal, Christopher Melchert
Ahmad Riza Khan Barelwi, Usha Sanyal
Akbar, André Wink
Al-Ma'mun, Michael Cooperson
Al-Mutanabbi, Margaret Larkin
Amir Khusraw, Sunil Sharma
Ashraf 'Ali Thanawi, Muhammad Qasim Zaman
Chinggis Khan, Michal Biran
El Hajj Beshir Agha, Jane Hathaway
Fazlallah Astarabadi and the Hurufis, Shazad Bashir
Ghazali, Eric Ormsby
Hasan al-Banna, Gudrun Krämer
Husain Ahmad Madani, Barbara Metcalf
Ibn 'Arabi, William C. Chittick
Ibn Fudi, Ahmad Dallal
Ikhwan al-Safa, Godefroid de Callatay
Imam Shafi'i, Kecia Ali
Karim Khan Zand, John R. Perry
Mehmed Ali, Khaled Fahmy
Mu'awiya ibn abi Sufyan, R. Stephen Humphreys
Muhammad Abduh, Mark Sedgwick
Mulla Sadra, Sayeh Meisami
Nasser, Joel Gordon
Nazira Zeineddine, Miriam Cooke
Sa'di, Homa Katouzian
Shaykh Mufid, Tamima Bayhom-Daou
Usama ibn Munqidh, Paul M. Cobb

For current information and details of other books in the series, please visit www.oneworld-publications.com

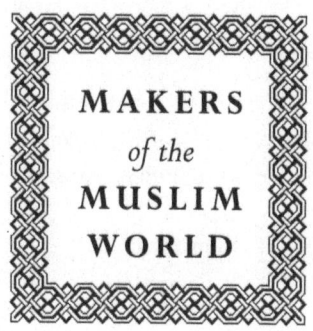

Ibn 'Abd al-Wahhab

MICHAEL CRAWFORD

IBN 'ABD AL-WAHHAB

A Oneworld Book
First published in North America, Great Britain & Australia
by Oneworld Publications, 2014

Reprinted, 2020

Copyright © Michael Crawford 2014

All rights reserved
Copyright under Berne Convention
A CIP record for this title is available
from the British Library

ISBN 978-1-78074-589-3
eISBN 978-1-78074-590-9

Typeset by Jayvee, Trivandrum, India
Printed and bound in Great Britain by Clays Ltd,
Elcograf S.p.A.

Oneworld Publications
10 Bloomsbury Street
London WC1B 3SR
England

Stay up to date with the latest books,
special offers, and exclusive content from
Oneworld with our newsletter

Sign up on our website
oneworld-publications.com

CONTENTS

INTRODUCTION 1

1 THE WAHHABI PHENOMENON 5
Contested Origins 8
Divisive Sect or New Orthodoxy? 9
Backward-Looking or Ahead of Its Time? 11
Religious Universalism and Political Particularism 13
Sources of a Controversial History 15

2 AGITATOR FOR GOD 19
Scion of a Small Town Culture 19
Regional Travel and Early Influences 22
Response to an Ecumenical Challenge? 25
Narrow Window on the Wider Islamic World 27
Relaunching the Campaign for Godliness 28
The al-'Uyayna Years 30

3 GUIDE OF THE COMMUNITY 35
Alliance with the Al Sa'ud of al-Dir'iyya 35
Overturning the Status Quo 37
The Battle for Najd 38
Later Career 41
Personality 44

4 CHAMPION OF TRUE BELIEF 47
Ibn 'Abd al-Wahhab's Writings 48
Assertion of Orthodoxy 51
Oneness of God 54
Tawhid in Action 57
Friends, Enemies, and the Fifth Column 58
A Community Apart 60

5 IDEOLOGUE OF STRUGGLE 61
Excommunication (*Takfir*) 61
Secondary *Takfir* and Emigration (*Hijra*) 65
Jihad 69

6 SCOURGE OF POLYTHEISTS 73
Sunni Clerical Opponents 73
The Bedouin 76
Customary Law 78
Takfir of the Bedouin 79
Tribalism and the Bedouin 80
Holy Men, Cults, and Sufis 83
The Shi'a 86

7 THE REGIME OF GODLINESS AND THE POLITICAL ORDER 89
Explaining the Genesis of Wahhabism 89
Social and Economic Trends 90
State Formation and the Regime of Godliness 92
Commanding Right and Forbidding Wrong 94
Government and the Political Order 96
Obedience to the Ruler 98
Princes and Clerics 100
Imamate 102
Administration of Justice 103
Social Justice 104
Conclusion 105

8 WAHHABISM, SAUDI STATES, AND FOREIGN POWERS 107
Saudi Expansion and Conquest of the Holy Cities 108
Spreading the Word 109
Destruction of al-Dir'iyya 111
Wahhabi View of the Ottomans 112
Saudis and Christian Powers 114

The Second Saudi State's Uneven Career 117
Civil War and Collapse of the Second Saudi State 119
Restoration and Renewal 120
The Ikhwan and Internal Dissidence 122
Senior Clerics Become Officials 123
The Nasserist Challenge and the Saudi Bid for Islamic Leadership 125

9 WAHHABISM AND RELIGIOUS RADICALISM IN SAUDI ARABIA 127
The Trauma of Juhayman 128
The "Awakening" 130
Jihadism 131

10 IBN 'ABD AL-WAHHAB'S LEGACY 135

Bibliography 139
Further Reading 143
Index 145

INTRODUCTION

Muhammad ibn 'Abd al-Wahhab aroused great controversy in his lifetime. Two centuries and more after his death in 1792 he still provokes strong, often passionate, views. For some Muslims he is the model of a religious activist who fought against the odds to establish a regime of Islamic godliness. For others, especially Shi'a or those associated with mystic orders, he is a hate figure. Some also see him as the ideological progenitor of Usama bin Ladin and the modern scourge of al-Qa'ida. Few would deny he has shaped the Muslim world.

Ibn 'Abd al-Wahhab created a remarkable phenomenon in the Wahhabi movement that is named after him. For over 250 years it has rested on the twin pillars of a clear credo and an unbroken alliance with temporal power. Absolutist theology and political and religious ambition made it the dominant force in Arabia. It transformed its champions, the Al Sa'ud (House of Sa'ud), from the petty rulers of a central Arabian settlement with a talent for balancing interests in the eighteenth century, into the guardians of Mecca and Medina (Islam's two Holy Places) and beneficiaries of some of the earth's greatest proven oil reserves in the twentieth.

Both movement and dynasty have endured many vicissitudes since the 1740s. For all the accusations against them of doctrinal and institutional rigidity, they have demonstrated both resilience and adaptability. Long experience of triumphs and bitter defeats has made the Al Sa'ud cautious in wielding the enormous religious, political, and economic power they possess today. Older Saudi princes have a strong sense of history. Others may have forgotten distant events in the Arabian Peninsula; they have not.

I became interested in early Wahhabism in the late 1970s when Gulf studies were in their infancy and the Iranian revolution consumed much academic attention. Saudi history was barely charted territory. My concern then, as now, was with the relationships between religious doctrine, political power, and events on the ground. Although this book focuses on the career, teachings, and impact of Ibn 'Abd al-Wahhab, in these pages he shares the limelight with the movement forever associated with his name, and with the Al Sa'ud who became arbiters of its fate.

Since this book is as much about early Wahhabism as about Ibn 'Abd al-Wahhab, I devote chapter 1 to a brief overview of the Wahhabi phenomenon. The next two chapters outline Ibn 'Abd al-Wahhab's background, career, and personality. The following three review his core doctrine of the Oneness of God (explained in chapter 2 and then in greater detail in chapter 4), its supporting concepts, and the main targets in society of his criticism.

Chapter 7 considers Ibn 'Abd al-Wahhab's stance on the regulation of society and government, and reflects on unresolved questions about the origins of Wahhabism: why then? why there? and why in that form? Chapter 8 offers an outline of the history of the three Saudi states, the first spanning the period 1744–1818, the second lasting from the 1820s until the 1880s, and the third in existence since 1902. Chapter 9 reviews briefly the ideological development of modern Wahhabism in Arabia, and its relationship with Salafism and jihadi extremism.

Concluding remarks on Ibn 'Abd al-Wahhab's achievement in chapter 10 are succeeded in the appendix by a short bibliography and suggested further reading on him, Wahhabism, and Saudi history. I have concentrated throughout on Wahhabism in Arabia and have not tried to cover the much wider subject of its manifestations elsewhere in the world.

I refer throughout to Muhammad ibn 'Abd al-Wahhab as Ibn 'Abd al-Wahhab. This is how he referred to himself in correspondence (e.g. Ibn Ghannam, 1949, 1:151). I also use the terms "Wahhabi" and "Wahhabism." Although at times Wahhabis have called themselves just that, today they treat the name as derogatory and reject it. They prefer *muwahhidun* (practitioners of *tawhid* or Oneness of God) or Salafis, a label that encompasses a broader spread of belief. Since "Wahhabi" and "Wahhabism" have become otherwise universally accepted labels, I shall use them – with neutral intent.

I have employed Common Era (C.E.) dates. Where the original sources supply a specific date in the Islamic calendar for an event,

I have converted it to its C.E. equivalent, using www.islamicfinder.org/dateConversion.php. Where they offer just a year, I have given the two C.E. years with which it overlaps (in the form, e.g., 1729/30), unless the context makes it obvious in which C.E. year the event fell.

It is impossible to be entirely consistent in the transliteration of Arabic names and words. Where place names now have a widely accepted spelling in English, I have adopted that in the text (e.g. Mecca or Riyadh). Otherwise I have adopted current academic practice (but omitted diacritics).

For ease of reading, I have restricted the number of proper names in the text to those that are essential. I have placed full footnotes online at: www.oneworld-publications.com/books/michael-crawford/ibn-abd-al-wahhab

I thank Professor Patricia Crone of Princeton (the general editor) for her initial help with this book, Professor Bernard Haykel, also of Princeton, and Charles Richards of London for their detailed comments. I am alone responsible for remaining errors. I owe a broader debt to Professors Haykel and Michael Cook of Princeton, and to Dr. Saud al-Sarhan of Riyadh for deepening my understanding of Wahhabism. For the record, I have not been beholden in preparing or writing this book to any institution, body, or individual for funding.

1

THE WAHHABI PHENOMENON

In mid-1798 Napoleon invaded and occupied Egypt, a self-ruling province of the Ottoman empire which then exercised suzerainty over much of the Middle East. Although some Ottomans had worried about growing Western advantage since the failed siege of Vienna in 1683, most Muslim observers were traumatized. A contemporary Yemeni religious reformer described this first Western occupation of Arab lands for centuries as making "the eyes of Islam and of Muslims weep" (al-Shawkani, 1929/30, 2:8). The imagery was conventional but the shock genuine and deeply felt around the region. The Ottoman sultan warned of a French descent on the Holy Cities, which he did not rule directly (ibid., 2:9–15).

The defeat by Napoleon of forces fielded by Egypt's mamluk rulers and then Nelson's audacious destruction of Napoleon's fleet at the Battle of the Nile were brutal demonstrations of the military and technological gap that had opened between the Christian powers and Islam's premier empire. Recognition by both rulers and subjects of the backwardness of their societies and inferiority – all the more painful because it conflicted with Muslims' conviction of God's favor and of their own superiority over Christians – triggered a long Ottoman reform process that lasted until the empire collapsed at the end of the First World War.

The political, military, and cultural impact of the French occupation of Egypt on contemporary governments and societies in the region has made it a favored starting point for Western histories of the modern Middle East. The ensuing narrative relates how Ottoman efforts to recover ground, lost both physically and metaphorically to

Western powers and Russia, concentrated first on revitalization of the military. As the nineteenth century progressed and the Ottomans saw that Western advantage stemmed from more than military technology and prowess, they extended the reform process under the broad heading of the Tanzimat to the political, economic, and social fields.

Subsequent modernization across the region, based on European models, was seen by its inhabitants as a reaction to Western pressures, and to be measured against Western benchmarks. Prominent Arab thinkers sought to adapt and liberalize Islam to assist the development process. Those engaged in politics after the First World War, operating in newly created nation states carved out of the old Ottoman empire, seized on European doctrines of secular nationalism to mobilize and justify popular hostility to colonial occupation and influence. Even major Islamist strands, such as the Muslim Brotherhood which first emerged in Egypt in the 1920s in parallel and competition with nationalism, reflected heavy Western influence as well as the effects of early globalization.

This standard account of regional history rightly presents Westernization as the key component and instrument of modernization across the Middle East. Yet modernizing reform in the region was not jump-started by the French conquest of Egypt. Contrary to the impression of eighteenth-century stagnation often conveyed by historians, the Arab and Persian worlds demonstrated a degree of political, military, and intellectual vibrancy even before rivalry between France under Napoleon and England detonated in a transcontinental war. Modernization began before Westernization and amounted to more than that.

By the eighteenth century dissatisfaction with existing approaches to government, religion, and military organization had already stimulated reformist impulses in Middle Eastern ruling circles. It had a similar effect among Muslim clerics ('ulama), who operated without any formal hierarchy of authority and were among the leading public intellectuals of their time. Some initiatives dissipated without effect. Others took hold and became fully fledged, sometimes radical, campaigns to transform the status quo. Historians have tended to see Wahhabism as typifying such movements. But its religious dogma was not representative of wider intellectual trends and its political and social activism expressed itself in an unusually aggressive form (Dallal, 2011, 108–11).

Wahhabism as an indigenous religious reform movement was born in inland Arabia in the mid-eighteenth century. It arose in the central Arabian hinterland of Najd, a region long disdained by Arab metropolitan elites as a religious and cultural backwater. It lay beyond the Ottoman orbit and remote from the hybrid port culture of the Arabian Gulf with its close links to India and East Africa. It belonged neither to the story of Westernization in the Middle East nor geographically to the worlds of the Mediterranean or the Red Sea and western Indian Ocean, where Muslim rulers first felt the modern political and commercial influence of European powers.

When from 1790 Wahhabism exploded out of Arabia to assume a disruptive role on the Ottoman stage, regional elites saw it as an inexplicable, almost anarchic intrusion from a deprived periphery. Some Western historians adopted this perspective, depicting it as "a solitary protest in a corrupt world" that exhibited features peculiar to the Arabian Peninsula (Gibb, 1947, 35). Many sweeping regional histories grant Wahhabism mere footnote status as an anomaly outside the main strands of narrative or analysis.

The early Wahhabi challenge to the political and religious assumptions underlying the Ottoman world can indeed seem curiously detached in origin from the rest of the Islamic world of its time. For all its religious inspiration and modern reputation as an ideology of resistance, it offered no transferable political model for Muslims facing political and commercial pressures from European powers.

The first Wahhabis of the 1740s appear to have been unaware of the speed and depth of contemporary English and French intrusion into far-off Muslim territories. Their better-informed successors remained undeterred by Napoleon's invasion of Egypt, or further English inroads into Islamic lands in India, from setting out to confound the Ottoman sultan, who had only recently reasserted his claim to be the caliph or leader of Muslims. It was not the French who launched themselves by sea at the Holy Cities of Islam but the Wahhabis. They encroached by land and captured them in 1803–6. As the sultan was officially guardian of the Holy Places, this loss, and the subsequent Saudi ban on the pilgrimage caravans he sponsored, dented his religious credentials and regional prestige.

This came at a bad time for the Ottoman empire. Its nerve center at the Sublime Porte in Istanbul was working to navigate the stormy waters of the Napoleonic War without losing more territory. The Wahhabis by contrast were committed to addressing the degraded condition of the Islamic world. Their targets were not distant Christians but Muslims in their own neighborhood. This divisive approach at a crucial moment in regional history fueled the controversy over the origins, objectives, and approach of the movement.

CONTESTED ORIGINS

The religious campaign launched by Muhammad ibn 'Abd al-Wahhab (1703–92) in the late 1730s, which found political and military champions in the Al Sa'ud dynasty, took decades to defeat local rivals within the confines of Najd. In the early 1790s Saudi forces, accompanied by Wahhabi preachers, occupied al-Ahsa (in today's Eastern Province) and started raiding into the Ottoman provinces of Iraq and into the Hijaz to the west. There the Hashimite *sharif*s of Mecca – descendants of the Prophet – ruled the Holy Cities for the Ottoman sultan. The Wahhabis saw this campaign as a summons to God and an invitation to act as instruments of God's power. The gathering pace of their territorial expansion, which to them signified divine validation of their doctrines, caused consternation among opponents.

Anti-Wahhabis were perplexed by the origins of the movement and the motives of its founder. They could not accept that one individual alone had supplied the creed and inspiration for this dangerous phenomenon. From the first they cast Ibn 'Abd al-Wahhab as an evil deviant who, for his own reasons or out of "whim", was intent on leading Muslims astray (Traboulsi, 2002, 402). They swiftly invented the term "Wahhabi" to denigrate the movement as sectarian, as having deviated from the path (*Sunna*) of the Prophet and his community. This was especially insulting to a man who railed against religious hierarchies that sought to intervene between God and the individual.

Much later it became easier to besmirch its founder as the agent of an outside power, especially the British, and to suggest that the movement even at its outset existed only to serve the covert aims of others. This notion gained particular currency in mystic circles in Turkey in the 1920s, just as the newly formed country was coming to terms with the loss of the pan-Islamic role bestowed by the Ottoman caliphate and the empire it had once led and dominated. Some Turks blamed the Wahhabis for deserting the Ottomans during the First World War just as they had allegedly betrayed them in Napoleon's time.

This line that, far from being a genuine indigenous movement, Wahhabism was the destructive creature of a hidden (foreign) hand is still reflected in anti-Wahhabi literature. One recent work, published in Tehran, capital of the Shi'i geopolitical rival to Wahhabi Saudi Arabia, has the self-explanatory title *The Wahhabi Sect: in the service of whom?* (al-Taqwa, n.d.).

DIVISIVE SECT OR NEW ORTHODOXY?

Controversy has always clouded understanding of how and why Wahhabism originated. Ibn 'Abd al-Wahhab contested the prevailing consensus of his era and earned the remorseless hostility of many local and regional clerics over his long lifetime. His raw challenge to the religious establishment of his era, and the political and military gauntlet thrown down by the Al Sa'ud to the Ottomans, earned the early Wahhabis a reputation for sectarianism, intolerance, and vandalism.

Much of the controversy was stilled by the Ottoman demolition of the First Saudi State in 1818, the withdrawal of the Wahhabi movement into the fastness of Arabia for much of the nineteenth century, and the skill with which Saudi ruler 'Abd al-'Aziz ibn 'Abd al-Rahman Al Sa'ud (known to the West as Ibn Sa'ud) restored its fortunes after 1902 and expanded his state's boundaries even before the First World War. No sooner had the Wahhabis recaptured the Holy Cities in the 1920s and placed themselves back at the heart of Islam than other Muslims again expressed alarm at the exclusivism of their creed and their intolerance of diversity in belief and practice. A fuller account of this history is provided in chapter 8.

Despite this unpromising reception, the Saudis contrived from the mid-twentieth century gradually and deftly to quell much of the furor over Wahhabism's theological outlook and hostility toward other versions of Islam. In subsequent decades the movement presented itself with increased confidence as part of the Sunni mainstream, with an outlook grounded in the beliefs and practices of the first generations of Muslims (known as *al-Salaf*). The growing strength and spread of this revivalist Salafi trend in Sunnism (of which Wahhabism was an early manifestation), the power of Saudi petrodollars and propaganda, and the spawning of more extreme Sunni jihadist ideologies shifted the perceived center of gravity in Islamic practice and belief to place Wahhabism, in the eyes of many, firmly within the bounds of Sunni orthodoxy.

Set against the early history of the movement, this transition was remarkable. It occurred so smoothly that until the last few years many Western commentators on Islam unfamiliar with that history took Wahhabi orthodoxy for granted. One author even declares that "since its foundation in the 1920s, the modern Saudi Kingdom has been considered a byword for Islamic orthodoxy" (Ruthven, 2004, 134).

While illustrating how effectively the Wahhabis reintegrated themselves into the wider Islamic community, this perception overlooks the rejectionist character of Wahhabism and the centuries-old religious debate it spawned. One disconcerted observer suggests the shift has been so profound that Wahhabism has become not just mainstream but the asserted orthodoxy in many Islamic states even beyond Saudi Arabia and Qatar, the two states officially Wahhabi in religious orientation (Redissi, 2007, 26).

The growing acceptance of Wahhabism suffered a major reversal after the 9/11 attack on the World Trade Center. Recurrent and widespread claims associating Wahhabism with the al-Qa'ida brand of extreme and violent Salafism were deeply unwelcome to the Saudis. The charge enabled accusers to tap into centuries of bitter disputation between Wahhabis and their enemies. It sparked a vigorous, even vicious, debate among polemicists, academics, and popularizers over the extent to which Wahhabis and al-Qa'ida shared a common ideology and approach.

Many of these exchanges shed heat, not light. Contributions appeared contrived, shaped by contemporary agenda rather than by a spirit of forensic inquiry into historical facts or doctrinal links. Critics tended to view Ibn 'Abd al-Wahhab's doctrines through the prism of current concern with Islamic extremism. They detached his teachings and actions from their own time and place. This hampered not only understanding of the ideological drivers shaping Islamic radicalization today but a balanced evaluation of Ibn 'Abd al-Wahhab's teachings and influence.

In contesting established patterns of Islamic thought from both within and beyond the Islamic consensus of his era, Ibn 'Abd al-Wahhab introduced a new ideological and religious turbulence into the Islamic world. Much of today's debate within Islam is conducted in terms that he helped to revive and popularize. One contemporary critic, addressing the wider issue of extremism, has described the apparent capture of religious modes of thought by Wahhabism, the broader Salafi movement, and their offshoots as "the Great Theft" (Abou El Fadl, 2007).

Yet the powerful influence of Wahhabism and Salafism, into which today's Wahhabis prefer for reasons of protection and propagation to submerge their religious identity, has yet to translate into ideological dominance across the Islamic world. The ages-old struggle persists between competing religious forces for the soul of the faith, each seeking to enlist in its support the enduring power of religion over the hearts and minds of Muslims.

If today's contest within Islam appears particularly acute, we can attribute this to the popularity of political Islamism, the widespread use of religious language in politics, and concerns over the impact of violent Islamic extremism on Muslim communities across the world. Wahhabism in its first manifestation as an eighteenth-century phenomenon helped precipitate this struggle by giving it a more confrontational edge.

BACKWARD-LOOKING OR AHEAD OF ITS TIME?

Much traditional disputation about early Wahhabism returns to the issue of "orthodoxy". This term applies awkwardly to Islam, partly because there is no central religious hierarchy to define what is, and what is not, orthodox. I use it, as others have done, for its familiarity while avoiding the term "heresy" as the antithesis of orthodoxy. Some have argued that the term "orthopraxy" better expresses the general emphasis in Islam on adherence to a code of practice rather than doctrine as defining membership of the Islamic community (*umma*).

A pluralistic culture in Islam has traditionally accommodated a wide range of religious behaviors and beliefs. It was just this elasticity of doctrine, ritual, and practice that Ibn 'Abd al-Wahhab challenged. He for one believed in the concept and obligation of Islamic orthodoxy. His theological stance made him condemn much of the Islam of his own time. He and his followers adopted an uncompromisingly rigorous approach to religious observance. They were quick to outlaw those they saw as transgressors from the faith. Their prescriptive model imposed tight criteria for membership of the Islamic community. It revived with immediacy the long dormant question within Sunni Islam as to who counted as a true Muslim, who did not – and who should be the judge of that.

This exclusivist outlook encouraged contemporary critics to view the early Wahhabis as harking back to earlier conflict-ridden eras. They dismissed them as insular and backward-looking – or just plain backward. To them the Wahhabis, coming from an unsophisticated hinterland culture, wanted to reimpose a simplistic outlook that hardly suited the complexities of the pre-modern Islamic world. This criticism, often expressed with a blend of condescension and exasperation, was understandable. Yet how is it that to our own eyes Wahhabism, even in its original eighteenth-century form, displays features that can appear decidedly modern?

By challenging the status quo and popular religion, Wahhabism engaged a constituency beyond traditional religious establishments and outside religious circles or groupings based on educational, hereditary, or spiritual allegiance. In addressing the beliefs and practices of the individual believer, Wahhabis set out to appeal directly to all Muslims regardless of birth or background. Salvation was open to all on an equal basis. Everyone was equidistant from God.

For Wahhabis there were to be no spiritual intermediaries between God and believer, no political hierarchies between ruler and ruled, and no social barriers to membership of the community of believers. Wahhabism developed its own religious hierarchy in Saudi Arabia, causing theory and practice to diverge. Yet this appeal to all Muslims and repudiation of mediation and traditional hierarchies became defining characteristics of broader Salafism. It led to a gradual sea-change in popular Islamic belief and practice over the twentieth century.

An outlook that looked retrogressive to many eighteenth-century Muslims exercises strong appeal today. This is perhaps because in Middle Eastern societies Westernization has stripped away traditional religious and social hierarchies and intermediaries. Social, educational, and economic development has discredited or marginalized forms of worship marked by faith in charismatic figures, popular rituals, or superstition. It has also fostered impatience with the juristic superstructure of conventional Islamic thought. By condemning or undermining these while expressing itself in traditionalist terms, Wahhabism appears to many Muslims a neat ideological fit for today's conditions.

Wahhabism in Arabia was never itself nationalist or anti-colonial, nor did it borrow from the ideological armory of the West. It was a pre-modern movement that arose before the most serious Western threat materialized against Islamic lands on the Mediterranean or in India. It can present itself today, as it has always done, as an authentically Islamic response to contemporary challenges. Some critics dismiss the simplicity, clarity, and absolutism of its dogma as anti-rationalist and intellectually impoverished. But these features reinforce its attraction for Muslims suffering social dislocation and seeking explanations and greater certainty within their own religious culture. It offers reassurance and a sense of purpose in a globalized world that has removed much of the individual's political, social, and economic protection from outside forces while stressing his or her capacity to make – and act on – his or her own choices.

RELIGIOUS UNIVERSALISM AND POLITICAL PARTICULARISM

This stress on the individual's path to salvation, free of mediatory constraints, is modern and meshes well with the internet's offer of direct access to other people and their opinions. It has, however, caused a splintering of beliefs that has affected the Wahhabi movement as much as other religious and confessional communities. Thanks to influences from other Islamist strands there are now various different versions of Wahhabism in Saudi Arabia. Even during the movement's monolithic phase that lasted until the mid-twentieth century, there was always tension within it between the universal religious message of its founder and the demands of political loyalty to the dynasty that safeguarded it.

Ibn 'Abd al-Wahhab's vision was of a universal struggle of ideas and beliefs, between conflicting religious and social norms, between differing visions of the Sunni community. By seeking to strip the faith back to its essentials and create uniformity of belief and practice, his message possessed a timeless quality with an appeal above and beyond the local circumstances and cultural heritage of his audience. He was addressing all Muslims, contemporary and future, urging them to reclaim the essence of the faith and purge it of corrupt accretions that had sapped its strength over the centuries. It was to stand in all places for all time.

As a phenomenon in history, Ibn 'Abd al-Wahhab's religious campaign was confined in space and time. To ensure its survival and spread he tied its eternal and universal message to the political cause of the Al Sa'ud. He exploited Saudi protection and support to create a regime of godliness. This was his great achievement as an activist, applying his precepts to the particular conditions of contemporary Najd within the framework of his arrangement with the Al Sa'ud.

This regime of godliness was necessarily local in application. Its broader religious appeal was restricted by association with the political fortunes of just one dynasty among many in the small settlements of Najd. This political linkage created obstacles to wider acceptance. It was a handicap as well as an advantage. The measure of Ibn 'Abd al-Wahhab's success as an ideologue and religious leader lies in how far he still managed to shape political, religious, and doctrinal developments in central Arabia and beyond, aided by Najd's geographical proximity to the Holy Cities. But for this outcome, Ibn 'Abd al-Wahhab might have remained an anonymous, at best peripheral, figure in Middle

Eastern or Islamic history, featuring on its geographical, political, and doctrinal margins. Correspondingly, without the appeal and legitimacy derived from a universalist religious message, the Al Sa'ud too might never have emerged as powerful historical actors.

SOURCES OF A CONTROVERSIAL HISTORY

Most historical sources accessible to us are supplied by the Wahhabis and Saudis themselves. This is partly because Ibn 'Abd al-Wahhab operated beyond the reach and records of Ottoman bureaucracy but thanks too to the grip achieved by Wahhabism in Najd. This limits our understanding of events.

Saudi forces gained a reputation for book-burning when sacking the towns of regional enemies. Yet the Wahhabis were much preoccupied with texts, especially the Holy Qur'an and key religious and juridical works, but more broadly also with grammar and history. However limited his own intellectual range and depth, Ibn 'Abd al-Wahhab established an industry of religious writing. He compiled some works himself and wrote innumerable epistles and letters, some of which have come down to us. The polemics of his enemies have fared less well. Many of them, influential at the time, have sunk from sight over the centuries.

The Saudi ruler encouraged the writing of a detailed chronicle by an Arabic specialist from al-Ahsa, Ibn Ghannam (d. 1811). This work assembles many of Ibn 'Abd al-Wahhab's key writings and letters. It was a major undertaking, written in an elaborate literary style that contrasts with the simple, fragmentary jottings of preceding and some later Najdi chroniclers. It reflects a strong ideological interpretation and message. This is history moving toward a goal in the service of the movement. Even the next major Saudi annalist, Ibn Bishr (d. 1873), writing a less religiously colored chronicle in the later nineteenth century, also with the support of the Saudi ruler, presents pre-Wahhabi events as belonging to an epoch of "ignorance" that prevailed before the movement took hold, just as the birth of Islam had been preceded by an era of ignorance. Ibn

'Abd al-Wahhab's claimed achievement was to end that history of ignorance within Saudi domains.

Early Wahhabis put their faith not only in the power of theological doctrine but in a doctrine of power. God was on their side. They were advancing as instruments of Islamic history, a role to be recorded appropriately for posterity. Today's Wahhabis and Al Sa'ud are just as concerned with historiography and seek to guard their early history against adverse interpretation or misrepresentation as jealously as they do their contemporary image.

Until the 1980s much Western understanding of the Wahhabi movement rested on these two chronicles of Ibn Ghannam and Ibn Bishr. More recent publications of all Ibn 'Abd al-Wahhab's writings and of other Najdi chronicles have brought fresh historical insights. These are supplemented by surviving (and accessible) religious opinions (*fatwas*), polemics, regional chronicles, and local documentary sources. Reflecting an upsurge of interest among Saudis in the past of their families, tribes, towns, regions, and country, a new generation of Saudi historians less committed to dynastic history has directed detailed research at specific localities, tribes, communities, or notable families. Much of the primary material they have unearthed casts new light on the political, religious, and social conditions of the eighteenth and nineteenth centuries.

Historians have often viewed the pre-modern and modern history of Najd and the Saudi states through the lens of Wahhabism. This new source material reminds us that this has been just one of the factors – albeit a major one – in shaping local society and determining the course of Arabian events. Ibn 'Abd al-Wahhab himself recognized the strength of competing influences. He and his successors struggled tirelessly to make his campaign the defining narrative of Najd.

THE WAHHABI PHENOMENON 17

Map 1 The Arabian Peninsula in the early nineteenth century. The shaded portion shows the area under the control or strong influence of the First Saudi State at the height of its power in 1808. (© William Facey/Arabian Publishing Ltd.)

2

AGITATOR FOR GOD

Ibn 'Abd al-Wahhab courted controversy. It then clung to him and his movement. Much of it still follows a pattern set in the first years of Wahhabism. Alive and resonant for protagonists, this format can appear conceptually static and stale to outsiders (Commins, 2006, vii–viii). Its overlay makes it vital to place Ibn 'Abd al-Wahhab and his doctrines and activities in their own time and setting. So this and the next chapter describe his home environment, his travels and education, and then his career, first as a lone activist, and later as guide to the emergent Saudi state.

SCION OF A SMALL TOWN CULTURE

Najd is a plateau that lies between Hijaz and the Holy Cities to the west, al-Ahsa in the east, and the Empty Quarter to the south, with Jebel Shammar as its northernmost region. It is the heartland of today's Saudi Arabia with its capital at Riyadh. In the early eighteenth century most of the settlements lay along wadis, especially Wadi Hanifa in the al-'Arid area. Neither they nor any part of Najd at the time were governed by the Ottomans. Occasionally in preceding centuries the *sharif*s of Mecca raided into Najd on their own behalf, for plunder or to impose taxes for a brief period. Conditions were too harsh and lines of communication too long for these interventions to generate permanent control.

Today we might describe Najd in Ibn 'Abd al-Wahhab's era as geopolitically *terra nullius*, ungoverned by any state. In central Arabia there was just a patchwork of petty principalities that were not states in a modern sense. The largest and most powerful of these was al-'Uyayna by Wadi Hanifa. The population of the town and its dependent villages may have come at times to about 25,000. It was in al-'Uyayna that Muhammad ibn 'Abd al-Wahhab was born in 1703. He came from a prominent family of religious notables who belonged to the prestigious sedentary Bani Tamim tribe.

Ibn 'Abd al-Wahhab's father was the leading cleric of the town, dispensing justice as Islamic judge (*qadi*) and giving opinions (*fatwa*s) on matters of religious law or ritual in his capacity as *mufti*, while his mother was the daughter of another cleric. Father 'Abd al-Wahhab was, in turn, the son of the chief *mufti* of Najd in his day, Sulayman ibn 'Ali (d. 1668/9), a key figure in Najdi chains of learning (Ibn Bishr, 1982–3, 2:328–9). Many of Muhammad's relations were *qadi*s and *mufti*s in other towns in the region, including uncle, brother, and cousins. Some of them featured among his sternest critics, marking the extent of his rupture with his own religious heritage.

Ibn 'Abd al-Wahhab's family and other learned lineages in Najd all belonged to just one of the four Islamic schools of law, the Hanbali school, named for the great jurist Ahmad ibn Hanbal (d. 855). This was the last of the four schools to be recognized by Islamic consensus as one of equally valid interpretations of the *shari'a*, a status reflected in the way religious institutions were organized. It was also the smallest of the schools. It had died out in Egypt by the early eighteenth century and its dwindling numbers elsewhere had left Najdis perhaps the greatest single concentration of Hanbalis.

The Hanbali school's career had been marked by controversy. Some of its leading exponents were quietist. Others refused to conciliate doctrines and practices of which they disapproved, and contested them to prevent their acceptance by Islamic consensus. This latter was the tradition to which Ibn 'Abd al-Wahhab belonged. Opponents relied on the Prophetic tradition (*hadith*) that the Islamic community (*umma*) could not agree on an error to validate the status quo. The early Wahhabis took this as legitimizing their challenge (al-Rumi et al., eds, 1978, *RS*, 115). They were executing God's will in stopping the community falling into error.

Drawing explicit parallels with the pre-Islamic period, Ibn 'Abd al-Wahhab and chronicler Ibn Ghannam described the state of Najd before Wahhabism as one of "ignorance" (*jahiliyya*) (e.g. Ibn Ghannam, 1949, 1:5). This hyperbole was calculated to sharpen both the definition of the Wahhabi message and the contrast between the conditions then prevailing in Arabia and those required for proper Islam.

By ignorance they meant the relative paganism of the tribes and the common people, not the educational poverty of Najdi clerics. Despite unpromising geography, the latter had preserved their links to the rest of the Islamic world in preceding centuries. The unruliness of local tribes had prevented neither regional travel nor the survival in Najd of an ordered urban existence. This was conducted modestly when compared with life in the great regional metropolises of Cairo, Damascus, or Baghdad.

This small-town existence was vulnerable to nomadic pressure and the vagaries of climate. Yet it endured, despite a fragmented political, social, and tribal structure. There was uneasy interaction, grounded in mutual dependence and antipathy, between townsfolk, oasis-dwellers, and the nomads who roamed the desert.

Wahhabism took root in this precarious small-town environment, assisted by the remarkable persistence of a living tradition of religious knowledge, refreshed by regional travel, within some of the settlements of Najd, especially in the localities of al-Washm, al-'Arid, and Sudayr. Hanbali clerics performed the pilgrimage (*hajj*) to the Holy Cities and journeyed to Damascus and Cairo. There they became affiliated to the main streams of learning within their school. This linkage centered on jurisprudence rather than theology. By the early eighteenth century it seems to have been weakening.

Although there is a record of one Najdi student in the seventeenth century criticizing religious conditions in central Arabia, most Najdis returned home, without ambitions for change, to expound Islamic law (the *shari'a*) in local towns. They wrote treatises, mainly on jurisprudence, and acted as *muftis*, often also playing the role of judges. This combined function was rare in the Arab world of the time. It enabled thinly spread scholastic resources to meet the demand for religious judges and guides across the widely dispersed settlements of Najd. It probably also encouraged conservatism and quietist subservience to political power, facets of the local clerical tradition that Ibn 'Abd al-Wahhab repudiated.

With sons succeeding fathers, either directly or indirectly, in their posts, families of clerics not only preserved a system of learning and justice in Najdi towns and villages but supplied much-needed continuity in government. In the role of intermediaries that clerics conventionally played in that era, they helped regularize relationships both within and between settlements. Communities, as well as rulers, looked to them to help resolve political and social conflicts, not sharpen them.

REGIONAL TRAVEL AND EARLY INFLUENCES

Heir to this tradition of learning, Ibn 'Abd al-Wahhab traveled to the Holy Cities and Basra as a young man. That he never reached Damascus, or, probably, Baghdad, the two surviving intellectual centers of Hanbalism, was something he was touchy about in later life. Lack of evidence makes the sequencing and timing of his regional travel uncertain. We can be fairly sure he never traveled further afield, as sometimes claimed by detractors to cast doubt on his doctrinal antecedents. They concocted fanciful travels in Iran and elsewhere that seeped into early Western historiography (Abu Hakima, ed., 1967, 17–23; Margoliouth, 1913–38, 8:1086).

The Wahhabi chroniclers offer a duller, more credible itinerary. They have Ibn 'Abd al-Wahhab performing the pilgrimage to Mecca as a teenager, spending time then or later in the Prophet's city of Medina. He then traveled to the ethnically and religiously mixed town of Basra before returning home to Najd, via the religious center of al-Ahsa on the Gulf coast (Ibn Ghannam, 1949, 1:26–8; Ibn Bishr, 1982–3, 1:35–7). Confusingly, the family legend, passed on by a grandson whom Ibn 'Abd al-Wahhab taught in late old age, relates that he went to Basra first and Medina later (Al al-Shaykh, 2005, 65–71, 83–5). The sequencing matters because it affects our view of possible influences on him before he first campaigned against what he saw as irreligion in Basra.

The balance of evidence suggests Ibn 'Abd al-Wahhab studied for some months in Medina early on and participated there in an intellectual circle headed by a well-known Indian, Muhammad Hayat al-Sindhi (d. 1751/2). This teacher from the Hanafi school of law pursued a rigorous approach to the study of Prophetic traditions (*hadith*), stressing a return to the sources, rejecting *madhhab* (school of law) partisanship, and condemning some popular religious practices (Nafi, 2006, 215–17). Although Hanbalis were few and far between, the radical outlook of Hanbali thinkers Ibn Taymiyya (d. 1328) and his pupil Ibn al-Qayyim (d. 1350), though a minority strain within their own law school, remained alive in the Holy Cities among those studying *hadith* (ibid., 214, 226–30, 234–5, 239–40).

Like fellow students, Ibn 'Abd al-Wahhab presumably absorbed this critical outlook and dissatisfaction with the religious status quo. This did not mean everyone in the teaching circle shared similar views on how best to address this and renew the Islamic world (Dallal, 1993, 342). Ibn 'Abd al-Wahhab's practical and doctrinal approach proved much more radical and confrontational than the routes taken by others, such as the great Indian reformer Shah Wali Allah of Delhi (d. 1762), who also studied under al-Sindhi as a mature pupil (Dallal, 2011, 118–20; Dallal, 1993, 351).

We lack a detailed and well-supported account of the intellectual connections between early Wahhabism and other contemporary Islamic reform movements. These would help us pinpoint those doctrinal elements that Wahhabism shared with other intellectual currents featuring a new political and social activism. Most of the parallel reformist trends elsewhere in the Islamic world rejected the dogmatism and exclusivism of early Wahhabism (Dallal, 2011, 111). Yet if transnational intellectual influences on Ibn 'Abd al-Wahhab were weak and home-grown reformist impulses absent from Najd, what catalyst changed him from callow provincial student into uncompromising preacher?

Ibn 'Abd al-Wahhab's early outlook may have been shaped by political as much as intellectual or spiritual experiences. We do not know which years he was in Medina. Throughout this period chronic political instability prevailed in the Holy Cities. Any short-term visitor gained damning insights into the vagaries of rule by the *sharif*s. Spasmodic, arbitrary interventions by the Ottoman governor in Jidda and the distant sultan in Istanbul, and the entanglement in local politics of ambitious clerics, were features of an insecure and oppressive political culture (Dahlan, 1887/8, 167–75).

Ibn 'Abd al-Wahhab may have been upset by the unfamiliar religious diversity he encountered. He would have witnessed for the first time the religious, political, and social influence of the mystic or Sufi orders. These did not have an organized presence in the sparse settlements of Najd. They were well established in the Holy Cities. The student encountered Sufis among both his teachers (al-Sindhi belonged to the Naqshbandi order) and his fellow pupils. He ran across them too in Basra, which he visited after a spell at home studying with his father. Various Sufi orders were well entrenched in the Gulf port town, where they benefited from the active involvement and patronage of powerful families of notables. Two major shrines close by were dedicated to Companions of the Prophet, which attracted visitations – and later Wahhabi vitriol (Ibn Ghannam, 1949, 1:13).

The relatively cosmopolitan port of Basra gave Ibn 'Abd al-Wahhab greater exposure than he would have had in Medina to the Shi'a, both Arab and Persian. These formed a large part of the local population, which probably numbered 40,000–50,000 in this period. His stay would also have brought him into contact with Christians and Jews for the first time. There were established Jewish and Armenian merchant communities in Basra as well as English and Dutch representatives of East India Companies, Indian traders, and even a longstanding Carmelite presence. Most local Sunnis belonged to the Shafi'i school of law.

Once a vibrant intellectual and cultural center during the Abbasid caliphate, Basra had become just another politically unstable town at the extremities of Ottoman control. The beleaguered Ottoman authorities were under sustained pressure from unruly and threatening Arab tribal confederations. As recently as 1697, the Ottomans had lost possession of Basra to the Persians for four years. A more settled period followed for Basra and Baghdad thanks to an effective governor of Basra, who succeeded his father as Pasha in Baghdad. In the early

1720s the Ottomans even turned the tables on the Persians and pushed the frontiers of their control well into Persia where Safavid rule was disintegrating.

A few years later the Ottomans faced a looming military threat from the brutally effective Khorasani general Nader. He made himself Persian regent in 1732 and overthrew the Safavids by installing himself as Shah in early 1736. In the interval he besieged Baghdad and defeated the Ottoman forces after first being pushed back. On the Gulf coast his forces retook Bahrain for Persia in 1736. This period, when Nader was at his most threatening, was probably when Ibn 'Abd al-Wahhab was in Basra, although he may have visited more than once (Al al-Shaykh, 2005, 65).

RESPONSE TO AN ECUMENICAL CHALLENGE?

We do not know what sparked Ibn 'Abd al-Wahhab's religious campaign in Basra. His writings do not cover or refer to this period, nor mention Nader Shah. Basrans may have been alarmed by Nader's run of military successes against both Sunni Afghans and Ottomans, achieved through new tactics and enhanced training for his troops. For Ibn 'Abd al-Wahhab, Nader's quixotic but determined attempt, signaled as early as 1734, to have a modified form of Shi'ism reintegrated into Sunni Islam may have appeared more threatening still.

Ostensibly Shi'i himself, Nader was driven by an ambition to govern a wide empire of Shi'i and Sunni subjects. He relied heavily on Sunni soldiers with no residual loyalty to the Safavids. He was keen to legitimize his own rule by undercutting Safavid-sponsored anti-Sunnism and set out to persuade the Ottomans that, shorn of practices most obnoxious to Sunnis, Shi'ism should be accepted as a fifth Ja'fari school of law. He wanted it to have its own pavilion in the Great Mosque in Mecca like the four orthodox Sunni schools (Axworthy, 2009, 161–73, 236–7, 256–8).

Nader presented this proposal to his own people rather differently from the way he did to the Ottomans. Characteristically he helped quell domestic objections to its formal pronouncement during his acclamation as Shah in 1736 by having the leading Shi'i *mullah* strangled beforehand (ibid., 161). This encouraged other clerics to acquiesce, despite the financial depredations they were already enduring. Many *mullah*s reacted by crossing the frontier into the Shi'i holy cities of Ottoman Iraq. By swelling the size and influence of the Shi'i establishment there, they upset the communal balance in the south and around Basra. Ottoman-governed Iraq replaced Iran as the center for Shi'i scholarship (Nakash, 2003, 15).

For many years the Ottomans as Sunni champions played along with Nader's initiative to have the Ja'fari school accepted into Sunnism until they finally rejected it in 1744 (Axworthy, 2009, 265). In the interval, those not privy to Istanbul's cautious strategy and worried by the Shi'i doctrine of dissimulation could see in this ecumenical initiative a dangerous, potentially successful, assault on the bastion of Sunni orthodoxy. Nader's proposal threatened a breach in Ibn 'Abd al-Wahhab's conception of absolute monotheism and the formal absorption into Sunnism of those he labeled unbelievers.

Both the time and place of Ibn 'Abd al-Wahhab's first campaign against polytheism, Basra probably in the mid-1730s, suggest, circumstantially, that he may have been responding at least in part to the immediacy of this ecumenical threat, as well as to Sunni anxiety at the influx of Shi'i clerics into Iraq. He might more naturally have launched his campaign on Najdi home territory rather than in the unfamiliar and religiously and culturally mixed town of Basra. There his aggressive preaching attracted some fellow thinkers but ultimately led to his expulsion (Ibn Bishr, 1982–3, 1:36–7).

There is a suggestion in an anonymous nineteenth-century account of Ibn 'Abd al-Wahhab's stint in Basra that he was backed by some Ottoman officials and notables but this is uncorroborated (Abu Hakima, ed., 1967, 16–17). Those tasked to preserve the peace and social and religious cohesion in a notoriously awkward frontier town would hardly have warmed to the destabilizing campaign of an outsider, especially when this appeared designed to sharpen confessional divisions. Either they hustled him out of Basra as a dangerous troublemaker or he was chased out by popular elements hostile to his sermons against Shi'ism, Sufism, and local religious rituals.

NARROW WINDOW ON THE WIDER ISLAMIC WORLD

After adventures that ruled out onward travel to Damascus, Ibn 'Abd al-Wahhab headed back to Najd via al-Ahsa, a region beyond Ottoman control with a substantial Shi'i population. This was governed by Sunni members of the powerful Bani Khalid tribal confederation, which included Shi'i elements. They were presiding over a brief intellectual flowering in al-Ahsa of both Sunni and Shi'i learning. They intervened regularly in the politics of Najd which, as an inland region, depended heavily on al-Ahsa both economically and commercially. During a stay that apparently lasted several months, if not longer, Ibn 'Abd al-Wahhab studied under various Sunni shaykhs, both Hanbali and non-Hanbali. He stayed with one teacher who was a senior figure in another school and later became a critic, although Ibn 'Abd al-Wahhab retained fond memories of him (Ibn Bishr, 1982–3, 1:37; Ibn Ghannam, 1949, 1:50–1).

These limited travels convinced Ibn 'Abd al-Wahhab that the religion of his era had become so polluted by idolatry and innovation that it was not proper Islam. His criticisms embraced the religious centers he had seen and many others, including Cairo, Hadramawt in Yemen, and Mosul in Iraq, that he had not. He was disgusted by the religious divisiveness and chronic political instability that characterized "ignorance" in Najd but equally soured by his experience, however narrow, of the outlying Ottoman world. He scorned most contemporary rulers (e.g. Ibn Ghannam, 1949, 1:184).

Though Ibn 'Abd al-Wahhab never left Najd after his mid-thirties, he had gained a negative view of the non-Najdi world that did not change over succeeding decades. Despite later correspondence with sympathetic regional clerics, he isolated himself from non-Najdi influences. His perspective on the wider world froze in time just as his doctrines cohered into a corpus that he never revised substantively.

Significantly the three regional centers of learning he had visited, namely the Holy Cities, Basra, and al-Ahsa, formed the heartland of early regional opposition to his teachings. Opponents there never mention previous encounters with him in the polemics that have reached us. The speed of their reaction to signs of burgeoning support for his religious campaign in distant Najd, a region they otherwise despised and ignored, suggests they may already have known something of his dangerous talent for agitation.

RELAUNCHING THE CAMPAIGN FOR GODLINESS

It was probably in the later 1730s that Ibn 'Abd al-Wahhab returned to his father's house. This was now in the settlement of Huraymila, twenty miles to the north-west of al-'Uyayna. The old ruler of al-'Uyayna, 'Abd Allah al-Mu'ammar, who had made the town the most powerful in Najd, had died along with thousands of others in a devastating plague in 1725–6 (Ibn Bishr, 1982–3, 2:367). 'Abd al-Wahhab fell out with the headstrong new ruler who dismissed him in 1727/8, and took up the less prestigious position of *qadi* at Huraymila, a town with a long history of bad blood with al-'Uyayna (ibid., 1:37).

Once back, Ibn 'Abd al-Wahhab started proselytizing among local inhabitants to the dismay of his elderly father, who had once extolled his oldest son's educational accomplishments to close associates (Ibn Ghannam, 1949, 1:25–6). Father 'Abd al-Wahhab shared some of his son's disapproval of some forms of local religion, especially dervish excesses, but was a quietist who disliked confrontation. Perhaps encouraged by his younger son Sulayman, who succeeded him as judge in the town and later became a dangerous anti-Wahhabi (as well as a personal embarrassment to his full brother), he compelled Muhammad to moderate his outspoken condemnation of local religious practices in his teaching and sermons and to suspend for several years his effort to institute a regime of godliness in Huraymila (Ibn Bishr, 1982–3, 1:37).

An element of disagreement between Ibn 'Abd al-Wahhab and his father may have been the latter's possible links to the Qadiri Sufi order. This was named after 'Abd al-Qadir al-Jilani (d. 1166), a Hanbali whose shrine in Baghdad hosted a major Hanbali center. Ibn 'Abd al-Wahhab refused to distinguish between idolatrous manifestations of popular religion and sober mystic orders such as the Qadiris or Naqshbandis (al-Rumi et al., eds, 1978, *RS*, 154). For him they all traded in some form of intercession with God which he saw as placing the intercessor on a par with God, a practice he equated with polytheism.

Forced by filial obligation to hold his peace and without clerical office, Ibn 'Abd al-Wahhab finalized his instruction manual, *Kitab al-Tawhid*, a shortish dry book devoted to the Oneness of God that he may have begun in Basra (this and his other major works are discussed early in chapter 4) (Ibn Ghannam, 1949, 1:30). He was fortunate in Huraymila to have access to his famous grandfather's library of religious works since books were in short supply among the scattered settlements of Najd.

Ibn 'Abd al-Wahhab described the Oneness of God (*tawhid*) as the first duty of the Muslim before even prayer (Rida, ed., 1999, 27). He identified two key forms of this: *tawhid al-rububiyya*, representing recognition that God alone was the creator, provider, giver of life and death, and orderer of affairs; and *tawhid al-uluhiyya*, the acknowledgment that God alone should be the addressee of prayers, supplications, sacrifices, and other forms of worship. There were no other Gods or mini-Gods who could act as intermediaries or intercessors (Ibn Ghannam, 1949, 1:176).

To make his point about the crucial role of *al-uluhiyya*, Ibn 'Abd al-Wahhab noted that even non-believers (*kuffar*) subscribed to *tawhid al-rububiyya*. He sometimes called this unbelievers' Oneness (*tawhid al-kuffar*): "Unbelievers, especially Christians, include those who worship God night and day. They are ascetics in this world and give in alms what they receive from it, isolating themselves from people in a monastery. Nonetheless they are unbelievers, enemies of God and destined for perpetual fire because of their belief in Jesus and other saints" (ibid., 1:177).

This dire fate was shared by professed Muslims who observed all the precepts and requirements of Islam yet prayed to a being or object other than God. Such conduct took Muslims beyond Islam and rendered their lives, property, and wives forfeit, regardless of whether they observed *tawhid al-rububiyya*. It was *tawhid al-uluhiyya* that brought the believer into true Islam. Anything worshiped in place of God was an idol (*taghut*) (Rida, ed., 1999, 20).

This was the core message that Ibn 'Abd al-Wahhab preached with renewed energy once his father died in 1741. He attracted followers as well as wider controversy in the area. One part of the Huraymila community swore allegiance to him. This was a town composed of different quarters and clans like most Najdi settlements, and it lacked an overall ruler. Such was the level of hostility to Ibn 'Abd al-Wahhab from another element in the town that he was lucky to be tipped off about an attempt on his life and to escape unscathed (Ibn Ghannam, 1949, 1:29–30; Ibn Bishr, 1982–3, 1:38). Huraymila remained a thorn in his side for years. It switched allegiances and acted as a base from which brother Sulayman and other clerics schemed against him.

THE AL-'UYAYNA YEARS

Ibn 'Abd al-Wahhab presumably deduced from his Basra and Huraymila experiences that mere teaching and proselytism would not secure genuine and lasting change in a community. He had to harness political power to his movement, power that would render him immune to the hostility and plotting of fellow clerics – though not to their relentless invective. He returned to his birthplace, al-'Uyayna, now no longer the pre-eminent polity of Najd but still strong.

Resettled in a town he knew well, where his family name had resonance and the ruling family belonged to the same tribe, Ibn 'Abd al-Wahhab worked hard to enlist ruler 'Uthman ibn Mu'ammar, who had succeeded his brother on the latter's murder in 1729/30. He worked through instruction and preaching to create a nucleus of supporters to help him resume the religious campaign he had started in Huraymila. It is not clear whether at this point he became judge as well as the town's premier cleric based in the town's main mosque. 'Uthman's initial goodwill was evidenced by the way he gave him his aunt Jawhara in marriage (Ibn Bishr, 1982–3, 1:38). Her guarantee of safety had once delivered Muhammad ibn Sa'ud, ruler of al-Dir'iyya, from a scrape in 1726/7.

Ibn 'Abd al-Wahhab intended to build up his local position with slow deliberation but a *fatwa* he wrote, perhaps while still in Huraymila, gained wide currency and sparked regional controversy after being distributed by his opponents. We do not have its text but it appears to have condemned indiscriminately, and probably intemperately, not just local holy men or those who worshiped stones or trees but all forms of intercession, including through mystics and the best-known Sufi shaykhs (Crawford, 2011, 150–1).

It was the way in which, in his declaration of excommunication or *takfir*, Ibn 'Abd al-Wahhab lumped together as unbelievers practitioners of pagan worship, Muslim dervishes, and mystics, even those who prized closed strict adherence to the *shari'a*, that aroused the indignation and hostility of many clerics. They (and critics to the present) questioned what gave him the authority to seek to exclude from Islam those with a different approach to worshiping Allah. It seemed perverse that he seemed most hostile to Sufi orders that were markedly moderate and respectful of Islamic law. Indeed he always reserved his greatest antagonism for efforts to accommodate and reabsorb divergent religious strains he considered subversive of core beliefs.

Najdi critics of Ibn 'Abd al-Wahhab alerted the prestigious clerics of Mecca. The *mufti* there of the Shafi'i school, to which the *sharif*s of Mecca belonged, issued a coruscating condemnation in 1743 (Traboulsi, 2002, 391–405). He was supported by fellow *mufti*s from the other three schools. One or two of the clerics declared Ibn 'Abd al-Wahhab of unsound mind and several urged those in authority to hunt him down and kill him (ibid., 408–15). No cleric based in Medina, where Ibn 'Abd al-Wahhab had studied, signed the condemnation. This was presumably a sharifian initiative. At this stage the Ottomans remained little troubled by distant ructions caused by an unknown provincial preacher.

Although polemics were to pour in from Mecca, Basra, and al-Ahsa effectively declaring him an unbeliever (so amounting to *takfir*) (Ibn Ghannam, 1949, 1:33), Ibn 'Abd al-Wahhab launched a fully-fledged effort to establish a regime of godliness in al-'Uyayna. With the support of ruler 'Uthman and his henchmen he imposed compulsory prayers, enforced the *shari'a*, including Islamic punishments, and collected Islamic tax (*zakat*). Notoriously he imposed the punishment of stoning on a woman who insisted, in a brazen challenge to him, on confessing to adultery (ibid., 2:2; Ibn Bishr, 1982–3, 1:39). Although he tried to persuade her to retract, she refused and so he sentenced her to stoning, defying the contention of some clerics that, in the absence of a supreme head of the Islamic community (*imam*), it was impermissible to impose the strictest penalties of the *shari'a* (Ibn Ghannam, 1949, 1:203, 207).

Ibn 'Abd al-Wahhab attacked manifestations of popular religion, cut down trees worshiped by locals, banned exploitation of magic and superstition, and destroyed tombs that were objects of visitation. In a particular *cause célèbre* he and 'Uthman's forces demolished a tomb said to be that of Zayd ibn al-Khattab, one of the Prophet's Companions, at al-Jubayla near al-'Uyayna in 1742/3. This move caused outrage in the Holy Cities and elsewhere (Ibn Bishr, 1982–3, 1:39). Ibn 'Abd al-Wahhab abhorred such tombs as they encouraged veneration of the dead while enabling locals to profit from the gullibility of others. In this case he believed locals had wrongly designated the tomb as Zayd's so they could fleece visiting devotees (Ibn Ghannam, 1949, 1:123).

Under 'Uthman's protection Ibn 'Abd al-Wahhab assembled a vanguard of supporters among local notables from al-'Uyayna and neighboring towns, especially al-Dir'iyya where two brothers of ruler Muhammad ibn Sa'ud joined the movement (ibid., 1:31, 2:4). Even the latter's young son 'Abd al-'Aziz (b. 1719/20) showed interest (ibid., 1:222–7). Elsewhere, by the Wahhabi account, early Wahhabis were hounded by local rulers. These drew encouragement from condemnations that arrived from the religious establishment in Mecca, a prolific Sufi opponent in Basra, and Ibn 'Afaliq (d. 1750), a senior Hanbali based at the Bani Khalid capital at al-Mubarraz next to al-Hasa (ibid., 1:31–2). Chronicler Ibn Ghannam stresses at length the trials which Ibn 'Abd al-Wahhab and his followers underwent at this period, in terms reminiscent of the earlier experiences of the Prophet and Ibn Hanbal (ibid., 1:33–4, 37–8).

In the end 'Uthman came under direct pressure from the Bani Khalid rulers of al-Ahsa. They threatened to deprive the ruling Al Mu'ammar of the sizeable income from their estates there unless he killed or ejected Ibn 'Abd al-Wahhab (Ibn Bishr, 1982–3, 1:39–41). Ibn 'Afaliq offered justification by challenging the latter's right and qualifications to overthrow centuries of Islamic thought and writings. Having harbored Ibn 'Abd al-Wahhab for two years and enforced the regime of godliness, which the *shaykh* had promised would deliver him worldly success, 'Uthman gave way. Rather than kill him, which he said he could not do in the light of their past friendship and marriage connection, he had Ibn 'Abd al-Wahhab escorted safely to the neighboring town of al-Dir'iyya in 1744/5 (ibid., 1:40–1).

After a series of dispiriting setbacks the *shaykh* had finally found his haven and the instruments for his ultimate triumph.

3

GUIDE OF THE COMMUNITY

In the settlement of al-Dir'iyya where he sought refuge in 1744/5, Ibn 'Abd al-Wahhab made the gradual transition from tireless agitator to the revered guide of a developing political entity and burgeoning religious establishment. His role evolved over decades and with it the shape of the Saudi state. Neither he nor the Al Sa'ud had a blueprint for transforming a local regime of godliness into an expansive, unbounded empire. That was the outcome of a long, debilitating contest between the Saudis and their enemies, and of Wahhabi and Saudi responses to a range of religious, political, social, and military challenges.

ALLIANCE WITH THE AL SA'UD OF AL-DIR'IYYA

Ibn 'Abd al-Wahhab's transfer from al-'Uyayna to al-Dir'iyya in 1744/5 placed ruler Muhammad ibn Sa'ud on the spot. He knew giving Ibn 'Abd al-Wahhab refuge would bring him into conflict with the Bani Khalid in al-Ahsa and with other towns in Najd, and could cause unrest even within al-Dir'iyya. The judge of the town considered Ibn 'Abd al-Wahhab too extreme in his views and many in the settlement practiced popular religious rites of the kind Ibn 'Abd al-Wahhab abhorred (Ibn Ghannam, 1949, 1:7–8). Influenced by his wife, brothers, and oldest son, the conventionally minded ruler backed the new arrival.

This fateful decision committed the ruler and his clan to decades of struggle. Ibn Bishr suggests it issued from one historic encounter between the two that occurred within days of Ibn ʿAbd al-Wahhab's arrival at the house of a pro-Wahhabi notable. The *shaykh* promised the ruler earthly success provided he abandoned non-Islamic taxes and committed himself to *tawhid*. He told him that whoever adhered to *tawhid*, acted on it, and supported it would master both country and people. All of Najd was united upon "polytheism, ignorance, divisiveness, disagreement, and fighting one another" (Ibn Bishr, 1982–3, 1:42).

According to Ibn Bishr, the *shaykh* hoped Muhammad ibn Saʿud would become an *imam* (in the sense of leader of the Islamic community) on whom the Muslims would agree, and his line after him. He then explained Islam, the prescriptions of the *shariʿa*, and the need to fight for *tawhid* (he did not mention *jihad* explicitly). In turn the ruler asked the *shaykh* to pledge himself to that campaign, which he did to the last drop of blood. Other rulers imposed non-canonical taxes on their subjects, but Ibn ʿAbd al-Wahhab required Muhammad ibn Saʿud to forswear such burdens on the people of al-Dirʿiyya. Booty should compensate for resulting loss of income. The ruler duly gave his word (ibid., 1:42–3).

The much earlier chronicler Ibn Ghannam recounts no such definitive pact. He reports that at that first meeting all the ruler requested in return for a haven for the *shaykh* and his family was an undertaking from Ibn ʿAbd al-Wahhab that he settle for good in al-Dirʿiyya and not leave. Ibn ʿAbd al-Wahhab acceded readily (Ibn Ghannam, 1949, 2:3). It was as simple as that, without more elaborate terms. Non-Wahhabi chronicles of the era do not refer either to a specific pact or even to the existence of the Wahhabi–Saudi alliance at this point.

We may infer that the bond between *shaykh* and ruler developed more slowly and less dramatically than Ibn Bishr described, and was only later embodied in the legend of one decisive, resonant encounter. Ibn Bishr (d. 1873) was writing during an extended period of civil strife between the four rival sons of Saudi Imam Faysal (d. 1865). He had cause to stress political unity under one Saudi "*imam*" (a title the Saudi ruler assumed much later during the First Saudi State), and that successful exercise of political power depended on its alignment with true religion. This was a period when, in defiance of Wahhabi values, raw personal ambition and opportunism were tearing the Saudi state apart. Ibn Bishr was imposing retrospectively a symbolic framework on political arrangements that in reality evolved less tidily over a century before.

OVERTURNING THE STATUS QUO

The alliance with the Al Sa'ud after Ibn 'Abd al-Wahhab's three previous false starts has obscured the pre-Saudi history of early Wahhabism and the degree to which it generated local and regional controversy even before the Al Sa'ud became its champions.

Wahhabism was a radical movement in origin. It was directed at changing the religious and social status quo. On its own it did not seek directly to overthrow political arrangements by force. Opponents worked initially to crush it by enlisting senior clerics to contest Ibn 'Abd al-Wahhab's religious credentials. They hounded local Wahhabis, wielding the weapon of excommunication against them (Crawford, 2011, 151–4). They turned to local rulers to eliminate the movement as the *sharif*s of Mecca lacked the resources, and the Ottomans the will, to tackle a distant and apparently transient phenomenon.

These local rulers were unresponsive to arcane theological arguments. So anti-Wahhabis spread rumors of Wahhabi subversion and disloyalty to worry them (Ibn Ghannam, 1949, 1:32). They claimed Wahhabis planned to unseat them because of the non-Islamic taxes they levied, their conduct of government, and even their personal morals. Rulers were susceptible to warnings of subversion. They had few resources to help them preserve order and prosperity across the quarters and settlements for which they were responsible. Social and political divisions grounded in tribal or clan loyalties always threatened disorder. Ibn 'Abd al-Wahhab's apparently wanton encouragement of dissension within, and between, settlements was deeply unwelcome. He did not conceal his seditious view that local rulers, the Al Sa'ud apart, were oppressive, ignorant of Islam, and unable to tell right from wrong (ibid., 1:184).

It is telling that in epistles clerics are the main targets of Ibn 'Abd al-Wahhab's ire, not the rulers themselves. In his eyes the duty of clerics in settlements was to advise rulers and ensure proper religious observance. Clerics were privileged in society and carried a heavy burden of responsibility. Yet they did not understand their religion, obligations, or role. Religious knowledge had no value unless properly deployed. If not acted on, it amounted to mere ignorance (ibid., 1:181).

Ibn 'Abd al-Wahhab declared that the degeneracy of clerics and their readiness to compromise with both rulers and populace corrupted the people. Clerics should not be cowed by rulers, the weight of opinion in towns, or the pernicious popularity of holy men who preyed on the ignorance of common people. A regular refrain in Ibn 'Abd al-Wahhab's writings is the extent to which people's livelihoods were consumed by the greed of oppressive rulers. He also railed against those who exploited idolatry and superstition for personal gain (for example, by selling talismans and amulets, or purveying magic), a charge he directed at Sulayman ibn Suhaym (d. 1767), his clerical enemy in Riyadh (ibid., 1:229, 114, 139).

The most notorious of the local holy men was Taj (meaning literally "crown" or Sufi turban), a blind man based in al-Kharj to the south. He was said to have walked unaccompanied to al-Dir'iyya and other towns to officiate over popular religious practices for money (ibid., 1:8). He had so many followers that rulers would not interfere with his activities. Ibn 'Abd al-Wahhab was disgusted by their passivity and that of clerics in the face of such irreligion. Their desire for a quiet life in this world would lead to eternal hellfire in the next.

THE BATTLE FOR NAJD

The early Wahhabis were initially protected by 'Uthman ibn Mu'ammar in al-'Uyayna. They were persecuted in other settlements (apart from al-Dir'iyya). Once subject to excommunication (*takfir*), a weapon Ibn 'Abd al-Wahhab had been the first to wield against holy men and mystics, they were exposed to loss of lives and property. This experience of suffering harked back to the trials, imprisonment, and persecution of early Hanbalis, including Ibn Hanbal himself, and shaped the collective Wahhabi memory, as reflected in the reminiscences decades later of ruler

'Abd al-'Aziz (Ibn Ghannam, 1949, 1:144–5; Ibn Qasim, ed., 1996–9, 2:171–3, 1:262). Late 1749 saw the traumatic episode when the *sharif* of Mecca imprisoned the Najdis who performed the annual pilgrimage to Mecca. Some died (Ibn Bishr, 1982–3, 1:59–60). Ibn 'Abd al-Wahhab considered such persecution inevitable. For him capitulation by individual Wahhabis was illegitimate, save in circumstances of extreme physical duress (al-Rumi et al., eds, 1978, *RS*, 272–3).

Once the Al Sa'ud made al-Dir'iyya a haven, Wahhabis from other towns took refuge there. These included dissenters from the Mu'ammar clan in al-'Uyayna who had sworn allegiance to the *shaykh* (Ibn Ghannam, 1949, 2:4). This influx added to social strains and economic pressures within the town, causing severe distress. Despite working hard for a living, local Wahhabis and the newcomers took religious instruction from Ibn 'Abd al-Wahhab (Ibn Bishr, 1982–3, 1:43). They appear to have supported a renewed campaign to impose the regime of godliness but his emphasis this time was on inculcating the rudiments of the faith as he saw them (Ibn Ghannam, 1949, 2:4; Ibn Bishr, 1982–3, 1:44–5).

We do not know when Ibn 'Abd al-Wahhab supplanted or removed the *qadi* of al-Dir'iyya and his son. They were among those that sympathized with his aims but disliked his uncompromising posture and methods. Their correspondence while Ibn 'Abd al-Wahhab was still in al-'Uyayna had become increasingly ill-tempered (Crawford, 2011, 158). The two clerics presumably moved on swiftly of their own accord.

The nucleus of Wahhabi supporters retreated to al-Dir'iyya from other settlements while Ibn 'Abd al-Wahhab consolidated his position. They formed the vanguard for the insurgency launched by the Al Sa'ud against other towns. While still in al-'Uyayna Ibn 'Abd al-Wahhab had responded to *takfir* of the Wahhabis with defensive *jihad* (al-Rumi et al., eds, 1978, *RS*, 158). He had not sought to overthrow local rulers in other towns by force or launch an armed insurgency. Nor had 'Uthman used force outside his dominions in the Wahhabi cause. Instead 'Uthman succumbed to outside (and probably internal) pressure rather than risk an attack from the Bani Khalid in al-Ahsa, who controlled some of the town's most vital trade routes (Crawford, 2011, 159–60).

Ibn 'Abd al-Wahhab may have deduced that he needed the backing of political power not only to change the local religious and social status quo but to expand Wahhabism's territorial base so it could not be throttled by external pressure. First he consolidated his position in al-Dir'iyya by indoctrinating local inhabitants and Wahhabi refugees. Then he wrote to the rulers and clerics of other towns calling on them to follow true Islam. He had not taken this step in al-'Uyayna but it was a necessary precondition for offensive *jihad*. Some accepted the Wahhabi message. More rejected it and accused him of ignorance or sorcery (Ibn Bishr, 1982–3, 1:45).

Dahham ibn Dawwas, the tough ruler of Riyadh, sparked off conflict by trying to take nearby Manfuha, which his father had once ruled, after it joined the Wahhabis. On Ibn Ghannam's account, the issue seems to have been about political loyalties as much as religious allegiance (Ibn Ghannam, 1949, 2:4–8). Ibn Bishr places this first clash after the *shaykh*'s declaration of offensive *jihad* against opponents in 1746, a year or two after arriving in al-Dir'iyya (Ibn Bishr, 1982–3, 1:45–6, 48). Whether or not the outbreak of conflict was initiated by the Wahhabis, it was predetermined by their uncompromising doctrines.

In intensity and duration the ensuing struggle went beyond the periodic internecine warfare between settlements that was the long-established pattern, especially at times of hardship caused by plague, drought, or floods. This new contest was often desperate. In Najd it lasted much of the rest of Ibn 'Abd al-Wahhab's life. By his death in 1792 the Saudis were already pushing into the Hijaz. This long drawn-out, intermittent campaign ended in their capture of the Holy Cities and ultimately in an Ottoman-instigated intervention that proved catastrophic for the Wahhabis.

Initially the battles between al-Dir'iyya and hostile neighbors were small-scale skirmishes and ambushes involving few on either side. Gradually the struggle involved more settlements and greater numbers. Al-Dir'iyya's main antagonist remained its close neighbor Riyadh. In the 1820s this was to become the next Saudi capital. The feud between the Saudis in al-Dir'iyya and Dahham in Riyadh lasted twenty years. It inflicted heavy casualties (2,300 dead from Riyadh, and 1,700 from al-Dir'iyya, according to Ibn Bishr (ibid., 1:120)). Until Dahham and Riyadh were crushed finally in 1773–4, the Wahhabis could not rest.

LATER CAREER

Ibn Bishr tells us that, while old-style ruler Muhammad ibn Sa'ud lived and until the final defeat of Dahham, Ibn 'Abd al-Wahhab stayed at the heart of Saudi government and decision-making (ibid., 1:46, 182, 184). Chapter 7 looks more closely at the division of responsibilities between *shaykh* and ruler in those early years. The chronicler is explicit that the former had the final word in early operations and managed the state treasury. "No army rode and no opinion issued from Muhammad and [successor] 'Abd al-'Aziz save on his say-so and view" (ibid., 1:46).

It was only with Riyadh's final capitulation that Ibn 'Abd al-Wahhab relinquished affairs of state and control of the treasury into the hands of Muhammad's son, 'Abd al-'Aziz (d. 1803). The *shaykh* had taught him and he proved the model Saudi ruler. Even then 'Abd al-'Aziz still sought his endorsement of important decisions (ibid., 1:47). Nothing in Saudi or Wahhabi sources suggests that once the *shaykh* assumed a backseat, 'Abd al-'Aziz inaugurated an era of greater Saudi militancy driven by material ambitions. *Shaykh* and ruler, teacher and pupil, remained in close and effective collaboration.

Not many years after the original launch of offensive *jihad* by Ibn 'Abd al-Wahhab, he starts receding into the background in the chronicles. These focus on the military activities of the Al Sa'ud and the tortuous political maneuvering of their adversaries. There are, however, three critical episodes after the alliance with the Al Sa'ud when he resumes center stage.

The first incident was the killing of the Wahhabis' first political sponsor, 'Uthman ibn Mu'ammar. As soon as elements of his clan started to desert him to join Ibn 'Abd al-Wahhab in al-Dir'iyya in 1745, 'Uthman entreated Ibn 'Abd al-Wahhab to return to al-'Uyayna. Having given his word to Muhammad ibn Sa'ud, the *shaykh* deferred to the latter, who declined to release him (Ibn Ghannam, 1949, 2:4; Ibn

Bishr, 1982–3, 1:43). Muhammad ibn Sa'ud was still content for the powerful 'Uthman to reenlist his forces in the cause and he let 'Uthman lead some Saudi campaigning (Ibn Ghannam, 1949, 2:7–8). 'Uthman proved unreliable and wavered in his loyalties (ibid., 2:9–10). He was pardoned by the *shaykh* after turning against the Wahhabis once but reneged again. Ibn 'Abd al-Wahhab told a Wahhabi delegation from al-'Uyayna, worried they were about to be eliminated by 'Uthman: "I want you to give allegiance to the religion of God and His Prophet, be hostile to those who are hostile to it and ally with those who are allied to it, even if your ruler is 'Uthman" (Ibn Bishr, 1982–3, 1:60).

Apparently encouraged by this, local Wahhabis assassinated 'Uthman ibn Mu'ammar in the main mosque at al-'Uyayna after Friday prayers in June 1750. Ibn 'Abd al-Wahhab was apparently unaware of the plot. On news of the killing he hurried to al-'Uyayna fearing an outbreak of disorder. He insisted against the assassins' wishes that one of the Al Mu'ammar succeed 'Uthman (Ibn Ghannam, 1949, 2:13–14; Ibn Bishr, 1982–3, 1:60–1). The *shaykh* was probably influenced by his marriage link to the family and the fact that future ruler 'Abd al-'Aziz had married 'Uthman's daughter. She gave birth the next year to his oldest son and successor Sa'ud (d. 1814). After further trouble, Ibn 'Abd al-Wahhab had no compunction in 1759/60 in riding to al-'Uyayna and ordering the destruction of the Al Mu'ammar palace next to the main mosque (Ibn Bishr, 1982–3, 1:84).

The fate of 'Uthman is instructive. For there is no evidence Ibn 'Abd al-Wahhab disapproved of his killing. In line with his formal doctrinal position on apostasy, he did not berate or penalize the culprits. This conveyed a salutary message to 'Uthman's fellow rulers. In al-Dir'iyya Wahhabism was a creed of power that treated rebellions against the Al Sa'ud by those who had previously submitted as illegitimate and tantamount to apostasy. This rule of obedience did not apply in those places where power rested with anti-Wahhabis. These the Wahhabis labeled apostates to be overthrown and killed.

In 1753–4 the Wahhabis were confronted by an alarming number of towns renouncing allegiance and aligning with opponents. Most prominent was the *shaykh*'s conspiring brother Sulayman. Ibn 'Abd al-Wahhab held a convocation of Wahhabis from all the settlements.

He reviewed recent desertions and defeats, and encouraged them to hold fast to their faith, repent of any wrongdoing, and recommit to the struggle. With God's support this would be rewarded with victory (Ibn Ghannam, 1949, 2:19). Saudi fortunes revived.

The last point at which the *shaykh* witnessed the new Saudi state under serious threat was in the years 1764–5, shortly before Muhammad ibn Saʻud died in September 1765 (ibid., 2:74). In October 1764, after a period of almost unbroken Saudi military success, powerful forces combined to seek its destruction. ʻAbd al-ʻAziz, who had long led Saudi forces in the field, had attacked the powerful ʻUjman tribe and taken nearly 200 prisoners. Seeking revenge and recovery of their men, the ʻUjman asked for help from the leader of the Ismaʻilis of Najran in the far south-west of today's Saudi Arabia, on the basis of shared tribal affiliation (Ibn Bishr, 1982–3, 1:92–3).

The Najranis inflicted a major defeat on the Saudis, killing about 500 men, including seventy-seven from al-Dirʻiyya, and taking another 220 captive (ibid., 1:94). The *shaykh* gave the distressed ʻAbd al-ʻAziz bracing encouragement. But the Najranis' siege of al-Dirʻiyya brought all the traditional anti-Wahhabis back into the struggle. That included Dahham. Ironically he had submitted to the Wahhabis as recently as 1763/4 and just lost fifty men fighting for them (ibid., 1:94–5).

One longstanding enemy of al-Dirʻiyya was the head of the al-Zafir tribe, long a thorn in the *shaykh*'s side. Muhammad ibn Saʻud and Ibn ʻAbd al-Wahhab used him as an emissary to the Ismaʻili leader. He arranged a truce to release prisoners on both sides and the Najranis retired home (ibid., 1:95). This change of heart left the Bani Khalid, who had joined the anti-Saudi coalition, and their allies, including Dahham, besieging al-Dirʻiyya but unable to capture it. A decade later, in 1773/4, the tables were turned. ʻAbd al-Aziz captured Riyadh (ibid., 1:120), doubtless to the delight of the seventy-year-old *shaykh*. The surrender in 1776/7 of the latter's brother Sulayman (ibid., 1:128) was sweet vindication.

The capture of Riyadh marked the point at which Ibn ʻAbd al-Wahhab withdrew from everyday public affairs and devoted himself mainly to teaching and preaching (ibid., 1:46–7). We do not know when thereafter he may have relinquished day-to-day religious direction and judicial administration into the hands of one or more of his sons. The old and frail *shaykh* is recorded as the ostensible author of a letter to the *sharif* of Mecca only two years before his death (ibid., 1:171–2). Ibn 'Abd al-Wahhab fell ill and died in June 1792 at the age of eighty-nine (Ibn Ghannam, 1949, 2:154), to be buried in an unmarked grave at al-Turayf in al-Dir'iyya.

We have little insight into Ibn 'Abd al-Wahhab's private and family life. He had six sons who survived to adulthood, all clerics of greater or lesser distinction. The oldest was 'Ali, so the *shaykh* was sometimes known informally as Abu 'Ali (father of 'Ali). He also had four daughters. We know he married his first wife at puberty and later 'Uthman's aunt. We do not know who bore his children nor when they were born, save in the case of 'Abd Allah (b. 1751/2) (Al Bassam, 1998/9, 1:169). The latter succeeded his father as the dominant Wahhabi cleric, was recognized even by anti-Wahhabis as fair and mild-mannered, and ended his days in exile in Cairo, having seen the invading Egyptians devastate the Saudi capital and single out his talented, uncompromising son Sulayman for execution (Ibn Bishr, 1982–3, 1:424–5).

PERSONALITY

The encomia to Ibn 'Abd al-Wahhab in the Wahhabi chronicles paint a conventional picture of virtue. They describe deep piety, dedication, humility, and asceticism in his personal habits. He inspired awe among notables but was kind and gentle with students. He was scrupulous not to benefit personally from his position and always generous to those who came to him in need. He left no money to be divided among his heirs, just debts (Ibn Ghannam, 1949, 2:155). He was magnanimous and forgiving in victory (ibid., 1:35).

The most direct sense of Ibn 'Abd al-Wahhab's personality comes from the letters and epistles we have, mainly belonging to his middle years. These are addressed variously to fellow Wahhabis, opposing or wavering Najdi clerics, regional clerics or notables, the inhabitants of towns, the Wahhabi community, and the wider Islamic world. Many are written to the educated elite but Ibn 'Abd al-Wahhab was ultimately addressing the common people. His letters convey across the centuries a distinctive and authentic voice, and an immediacy absent from the duller set-pieces (described in chapter 4) that he wrote for a restricted readership of clerics, propagators, and students.

These letters correct the one-dimensional impression that "his message was not dialectical or polemical, his style not emotional, but brief, threatening, to the point and repetitive" (Hopwood, 1982, 31). Although sometimes allusive in style (and elusive in meaning), the letters project a more rounded personality. They show him adapting emphasis, terms, and tone to his target audience, moving from the doctrinally complex to the conceptually simple, from classical formality to Najdi vernacular. The mood of letters ranges from calm reflection to extreme exasperation. Although most of his correspondence has an acrid flavor, it gives a sense of a powerful personality working to achieve lasting impact in a fractured society.

Preacher, ideologue, teacher, and polemicist of skill, he defined his theological and doctrinal stance early in his career with stark conviction, though inconsistencies of approach remained. In succeeding decades, as guide to the nascent Saudi state, he cast and recast his core themes to meet specific purposes or circumstances, adjusting tone and emphasis to match the situation confronting the Wahhabis but without altering or elaborating on doctrinal substance. Substantive modifications to Wahhabi doctrine came after his death.

Unwavering in his belief in himself and his own righteousness, Ibn 'Abd al-Wahhab comes across as personally modest and unconcerned with his own status, indeed without worldly ambition for himself and contemptuous of those driven by material considerations. Yet he was no impractical religious visionary in need of grounding through partnership with a ruler. Having schooled himself in politics the hard way, he could be highly pragmatic and effective in political affairs.

Historians remark conventionally on Ibn 'Abd al-Wahhab's ideological rigidity, less often on his tactical flexibility, although this is evident from mid-career. It shows during the initial period in al-'Uyayna. He tried to avoid confrontation with his enemies. Yet they contrived to instigate regional involvement and local conflict before he was ready. Later many of the primarily political decisions he took, mostly in consultation with ruler Muhammad ibn Saʿud, were astute. His capacity for pragmatism is well illustrated, as when he deputed the al-Zafir tribal enemy to negotiate a truce with the Ismaʿilis, despite having himself long condemned the al-Zafir as infidels.

Ibn ʿAbd al-Wahhab's combination of absolute belief in himself and doctrinal and personal austerity suggests someone with small empathy for those less driven. We can be sure he did not suffer fools gladly. Yet his rectitude and physical and moral courage inspired others and aroused great loyalty among followers. He repaid this by safeguarding the welfare of those who suffered for the cause.

The *shaykh* needed his full reserves of courage. His ideological outlook put his movement starkly at odds with the rest of society. He was radical, deliberately divisive, and aggressive in intent. In his view, if it took force and compulsion to achieve God's will, so be it. He had in the Qur'an the theological armory and in the Al Saʿud the political and military resource. Above all, he believed with the great U.S. abolitionist, Wendell Phillips (d. 1884), that "one on God's side is a majority". With divine support ultimate triumph was assured.

CHAMPION OF TRUE BELIEF

For regional opponents Ibn 'Abd al-Wahhab was the man from nowhere, geographically and doctrinally. Some portrayed him as standing tenth in a line of twelve religious troublemakers in Islamic history (Ibn Ghannam, 1949, 1:161). Others viewed him as without intellectual antecedents. The senior cleric who spearheaded the Meccan assault on him in 1743 described him, without naming him, as "a person from the [common] people" – someone of no standing who acted from personal whim and had not sat at the feet of the *shaykh*s (Traboulsi, 2002, 391–2, 395, 402). Religious knowledge could come only from being taught by *shaykh*s, not by treating the Qur'an as one's *shaykh*. Ibn 'Abd al-Wahhab was self-taught, an autodidact, by definition ignorant because he was uncertified by the learned men who transmitted knowledge in an oral chain going back to the original written sources. Some classified him as possibly mad, a traditional way of writing off someone accused of religious deviancy (ibid., 409, 411).

Regional critics castigated this subversive provincial preacher for presuming to interpret the Qur'an and *Sunna* without enjoying the status to exercise high-quality independent judgment in jurisprudence known as *ijtihad*. He was saying that every common Muslim, even one who lacked his modest educational credentials, could do this. Ibn 'Abd al-Wahhab did indeed assert that his *shaykh*s had not known and understood the true Oneness of God (*tawhid*) (Ibn Ghannam, 1949, 1:146). He demanded that every Muslim, female and male, study the Qur'an and *Sunna* instead of following the long-accepted view within his or her school, as expressed by its acknowledged clerical proponents.

For critics this raised the issue: if the individual Muslim could attain salvation without guidance from established authorities and hierarchies, was each Muslim now to develop his or her own personal version of Islam? That would fragment, not unite, the community and promote doctrinal, political, and social chaos. And what did the resulting vacuum of authority mean for past and present clerics and the whole panoply of Islamic learning over countless generations? Ibn 'Abd al-Wahhab seemed to suggest that, once they joined the cause, new and ignorant Wahhabis should label the greatest Islamic figures of the past unbelievers, and defy the current religious authorities.

The idea these clerics feared went back to the credo of early Islam. It was that the individual had a direct relationship with God without intervening religious hierarchy or intermediary. This became a salient feature of modern Salafism, of which Wahhabism was the major premodern manifestation.

With his followers Ibn 'Abd al-Wahhab hardly countenanced, let alone advocated, doctrinal anarchy. He had no wish to see every Muslim propagating his or her own views. For all his revolt against the prevailing clerical consensus he envisaged the regular believer being guided by a cleric – so long as he held the same core convictions as himself. Ibn 'Abd al-Wahhab was no pluralist.

He believed that right could lie with one individual who enjoyed God's special favor, in defiance of the rest of the Islamic community. This was not new in radical Hanbali thought (Ibn Ghannam, 1949, 1:144–5). Yet any successful claim to this singular status required a compelling message to motivate believers and serve as the rallying point for a model Islamic community. For Ibn 'Abd al-Wahhab that was *tawhid*. Even if every individual had to return to the original sources rather than accept Ibn 'Abd al-Wahhab's word for it, the Qur'an and Prophetic traditions (*hadith*) permitted one interpretation only: the unchallengeable primacy of *tawhid*.

IBN 'ABD AL-WAHHAB'S WRITINGS

Contemporary clerics were concerned that Ibn 'Abd al-Wahhab as an autodidact had not inherited his thought from his teachers. Opponents regarded his religious and scholarly credentials as too slight and his abilities as too pedestrian to justify his campaign to refashion religious observance in Najd and beyond (Ibn Ghannam, 1949, 1:32). Both at the time and later, they disparaged him as both scholar and author (Sulayman ibn 'Abd al-Wahhab, 2005, 8–9). A recent critique of Wahhabism comments scathingly that "all of his works are extremely slight, in terms of both content and bulk" (Algar, 2002, 14). Another analysis compares Ibn 'Abd al-Wahhab unfavorably with reformist contemporaries and observes that Wahhabism "lacks intellectual complexity and thus does not lend itself to much intellectual analysis" (Dallal, 2011, 111). Others complain of Wahhabi anti-intellectualism.

Ibn 'Abd al-Wahhab's formal output was limited. He was above all a preacher, teacher and activist. His set-pieces reflected both these roles and his doctrinal priorities. These were centered on matters of faith (*'aqida*) initially, and not on jurisprudence (*fiqh*). He turned to that later. Two features characterize several of his best-known early works. They are in the form of teaching aids or lecture notes, and he relies primarily on quotations from the Qur'an and *Sunna* to convey his message.

The earliest and best known of his formal works, destined for a limited audience of clerics, propagators, and students, is his first instruction manual, *Kitab al-Tawhid*, possibly started in Basra and finished in Huraymila (Rida, ed., 1999, 17–95). Six short chapters in the first part of the book are devoted in general terms to *tawhid* and its antithesis, polytheism or idolatry (*shirk*). The remaining sixty-one chapters judge specific beliefs, activities, and utterances as belonging on the right or wrong side of the line (mostly the latter). Ibn 'Abd al-Wahhab sets out texts from the Qur'an or *hadith* or both at the start of each chapter. He then lists in note form points for highlighting. Such is the weight of quotation and the succinctness of the propositions he offers as comment that his own voice does not come through strongly.

Kitab al-Tawhid is not the general and argued exposition on *tawhid* that its status as a seminal piece might lead us to expect. Its instructional format can be found in other of his writings. It sets the pattern for Qur'anic quotations and assembled *hadith* that marks much of Ibn 'Abd al-Wahhab's work. A book on the major sins (*Kitab al-Kaba'ir*), covering conduct within the community and relations among its members, contains only quotations (al-Rumi et al., eds, 1978, *'Aqida*, 2:1–63). Ibn Ghannam treats this as his second most important written contribution (Ibn Ghannam, 1949, 1:50) but such methodology made Ibn 'Abd al-Wahhab's thought inaccessible to later readers.

The best introduction to his thinking and polemical style is the extended epistle *Kashf al-Shubuhat* ("the Unveiling of Doubts"). It is listed by the chroniclers as among his most important works (Ibn Ghannam, 1949, 1:50; Ibn Bishr, 1982–3, 1:185) and dates to before 1750. This systematizing guide to Wahhabi disputation, addressed to the individual believer, is more discursive than *Kitab al-Tawhid*. It reflects the interests of Ibn 'Abd al-Wahhab as activist as much as teacher. The epistle, much used in propagation, explains to followers how to reply to anti-Wahhabi arguments. It offers a doctrinal armory for encounters. He declares: "You know that on the road to God on High there are inevitably enemies placed who deploy eloquence, knowledge and proofs. From your knowledge of God's religion you must forge a weapon with which to fight these devils ... The ordinary exponent of *tawhid* (*muwahhid*) will defeat a thousand of the clerics of these polytheists" (Rida, ed., 1999, 104). Small wonder opponents were concerned to safeguard clerical authority from such challenge.

Other longer works by Ibn 'Abd al-Wahhab include compilations of *hadith*, some abridgements, especially of works by Ibn Taymiyya and Ibn al-Qayyim, an abridged and an extended biography (*sira*) of the Prophet, and some Qur'anic exegesis (*tafsir*). In one or two of the works, commentary or elucidation appears to have been inserted indistinguishably into the text by Ibn 'Abd al-Wahhab's descendants. He also wrote on jurisprudence, as discussed below.

Ibn 'Abd al-Wahhab made no claims to originality. Indeed he would have regarded that as abhorrent. He often exhorted interlocutors and critics to follow not his words but what was in the books about the Prophet's teachings, the thrust of which was to him self-evident (Ibn Ghannam, 1949, 1:151). His books were grounded in a narrow and dogmatic literalist tradition hostile to speculative theology (*kalam*). They inclined to interpretative authoritarianism, and embodied a strongly prescriptive approach. They lacked the intellectual virtuosity of those Hanbalis he admired so much (especially Ibn Taymiyya, Ibn al-Qayyim, and Ibn Qudama) and even the range and nuance of some of his opponents. The limited nature and range of his formal output was a weakness that his immediate descendants and successors in the nineteenth century worked to redress. They expanded the corpus of texts, but without much extending the confines of Wahhabi thought.

ASSERTION OF ORTHODOXY

Opponents viewed Wahhabism as a sectarian aberration based on a misreading of the sources. Ibn 'Abd al-Wahhab and his followers saw their call for reformation as unfurling the banner of true Sunnism. Their creed was neither more nor less than the strict monotheism enjoined by God called "Islam". This was reflected in their terminology. Ibn 'Abd al-Wahhab and chronicler Ibn Ghannam talk of "the Muslims", or people of religion, faith, or *tawhid*. They are battling against polytheists, or the people of error, falsity, or corruption. Those who make a covenant with Ibn 'Abd al-Wahhab enter into the religion of Islam, become Muslims, or offer allegiance to the religion of God. Those who resile are apostates.

Seeing themselves simply as true Muslims, Ibn 'Abd al-Wahhab and his followers found the term "Wahhabism" (*Wahhabiyya*) disparaging. It highlighted the person at the expense of the message, implied parallels with Sufi orders or cults named after their founders, and suggested a new sect or law school (Ibn Ghannam, 1949, 1:51). If they were to secure the credal citadel of Sunnism, they could not leave sectarian labels uncontested. They wanted to share neither the image nor the fate of the Kharijites, an extremist Arabian group of anarchic bedouin in the first decades of Islam.

The Kharijites' uncompromising religious faith had made them treat outsiders as enemies. They had risen up against the caliph and an encroaching Islamic state, and been crushed. Muslims deemed them to have been so extreme as to have excluded themselves from the community. Constant comparison in the popular mind with these Kharijites tried Wahhabi patience for generations. By the mid-twentieth century the association had faded, only to be replaced in 2001 by allegations of a link with new exponents of violent extremism, al-Qa'ida.

The early Wahhabis trod a fine line. They claimed membership of the Sunni community so they could influence its direction and defend *tawhid* as the citadel of Sunni belief. Yet, like earlier Hanbali controversialists, they also contested the beliefs and practices of that community to stop them acquiring legitimacy through the Islamic principle of "consensus" (*ijma'*), one of the ways the *shari'a* accepted and licensed plurality. This Hanbali challenge had long tested other Sunnis' tolerance. Early Wahhabis went further in their rejectionism.

They stressed the ground they shared with other Muslims when it suited their claim to orthodoxy. Yet they presented themselves as breaking conclusively with the religious past of Najd and the prevailing culture of the wider Islamic world. Non-Najdi opponents compounded this perception of exceptionalism by characterizing Wahhabism as a sectarian aberration, nurtured by a barbarous desert culture far removed from their own civilizations. Their use of derogatory or exclusionary labels reflected longstanding practice in Islamic disputation. It also disguised their difficulty in finding a sound theological basis for condemning Wahhabi doctrines. It suited both sides in the polemic about Wahhabi orthodoxy to perpetuate this image of discontinuity and separation. This contributed to the lasting perception of Wahhabism as an isolated, stand-alone phenomenon.

A vital element in the Wahhabis' claim to belong within the Sunni community lay in their adherence to the Hanbali school, as one of the four acknowledged Sunni schools of law in a religion that is, above all, law-centric. The Wahhabis' formal stance was that they were Sunni in the foundations of Islamic law and Hanbali in the branches (Ibn Sihman, ed., 1925/6, 38). Ibn 'Abd al-Wahhab made little of the Hanbali affiliation when stressing, as a Sunni, the universalism of his theological message. But he insisted on it when regional clerics assaulted the Wahhabis' Sunni credentials (al-Rumi et al., eds, 1978, RS, 107, 40). He and his followers were explicit about their recognition of the other law schools and reverence for their founders (ibid., 107; Ibn Sihman, ed., 1925/6, 10).

Some regional critics at the time and later accused Ibn 'Abd al-Wahhab paradoxically of both being a narrow Hanbali and rejecting the great *imams* who founded the four Sunni schools. They wanted to detach Wahhabism from Sunni orthodoxy by claiming he had overthrown the whole panoply of Islamic jurisprudence. This contradictory approach reflected their difficulty. The Hanbali school, which blended law and traditionalism, was the only one of the four schools to represent both a theological stance and a legal system. Local and regional Hanbalis could be anti-Wahhabi. Correspondingly, a non-Hanbali in jurisprudence could be a Wahhabi in theology, like the Maliki chronicler Ibn Ghannam.

Hanbalis tended to share certain traits. Ibn Hanbal, the theologian who founded the school, was an expert in Prophetic traditions. These set down the model path laid out by the Prophet (called the *Sunna*). Hanbalis' grounding in these traditions inclined them to be literal-minded, uncompromising, and hostile to each of rationalizing theology, allegorical interpretation of the Qur'an, and esoteric aspects of Sufism. They saw themselves as protecting the Prophet's legacy, both within the community and against external threats, especially from the Shi'a. This defensive mindset marked Ibn 'Abd al-Wahhab.

Ibn 'Abd al-Wahhab's leading works were on credal matters (*'aqida*), not jurisprudence (*fiqh*). He could be highly critical of concentration on *fiqh* (Rida, ed., 1999, 183). Some opponents considered that he undervalued *fiqh*, which helped resolve practical disputes within settlements over personal relationships, property rights, and so on, in favor of theological and doctrinal issues that divided people. Yet it is misleading to describe him as working to reject classical *fiqh*, including Hanbalism, and replace it with focus on *'aqida* (creed). He wanted to readjust the balance between the two. Because he preferred in formal works to rely on Prophetic traditions rather than the opinions of earlier jurists, his writings suggest limited interest in jurisprudence, although he was well versed in this like any judge or *mufti*.

Ibn 'Abd al-Wahhab's approach to jurisprudence appears ambivalent. On the one hand, he repudiated the blind following (*taqlid*) of a given school's position, right or wrong. He disliked the partisanship this represented, describing the practice as "the greatest principle of all the infidels from the first to the last" (ibid., 126). On the other, he never explained his approach to legal methodology systematically, although the issue of *ijtihad* was central to disputes over his credentials and rejection of *taqlid*. He left it to his pupil and son-in-law Hamad ibn Nasir to expound the classical Wahhabi position on *ijtihad* and *taqlid* (Rida, ed., 1928, 2(3):2–30).

Ibn 'Abd al-Wahhab's own exercise of *ijtihad* was extremely narrow. He urged others to adopt the position within any of the four schools of law that was most closely based on the Qur'an and *Sunna*. Yet he himself fell back on the regular, available Hanbali texts derived from the works of Ibn Qudama (d. 1223) that constituted the Najdi tradition in jurisprudence. He did not seek to liberate himself from this conservative legal tradition to which his forebears and contemporaries belonged. Rather he labored to abridge two derivative works based on Ibn Qudama (al-Rumi et al., eds, 1978, *Fiqh*, 1). Even this had a controversial reception in Najd. It appeared to slight two later manuals, on which most contemporary clerics with their restricted access to books had to rely (Ibn Bishr, 1982–3, 1:185) (and which were still approved for use by Saudi judges as late as 1936).

This hidebound approach to jurisprudence appears strikingly at odds with Ibn 'Abd al-Wahhab's broader radicalism. He had at his disposal the conceptual basis for jettisoning the juristic superstructure that developed from the third century after the Prophet. Yet he was content to perpetuate a local juristic tradition with relatively few followers beyond Najd. This, and the inconsistency it entailed, may have lowered clerical resistance to his campaign in Najd. But it also reduced Wahhabism's wider intellectual appeal and capacity for renewal and adaptation. A like caution or lack of intellectual curiosity marked how he tackled governance, with similar results.

ONENESS OF GOD

For Ibn 'Abd al-Wahhab the key criterion for the true Muslim was that he practised and enforced *tawhid*. This went beyond mere formal declaration of belief in one God whose Prophet is Muhammad. That pronouncement, known as the *shahada*, is the first obligation of every Muslim. As noted in chapter 2, Ibn 'Abd al-Wahhab identified two vital forms of *tawhid*: *al-rububiyya*, representing recognition that God alone is the creator and orderer of the world; and *al-uluhiyya*, the acknowledgment that God alone should be the addressee and object of worship. Although the two forms of *tawhid* were interlocking and indivisible, it was *al-uluhiyya* that marked true believers. These were known as the people of *tawhid* or *muwahhidun*, the term the early Wahhabis used most to describe themselves when they did not call themselves simply "the Muslims".

To Ibn 'Abd al-Wahhab the very terms of the *shahada* invalidated all intercessors. Practices involving an intermediary between God and man, such as praying to the dead, sacrifices to a saint or holy man, or the preparation of talismans or amulets, amounted to a serious form of polytheism or associationism (*shirk*) (Rida, ed., 1999, 177). The culprit merited expulsion from the community and exposure to *jihad*, unless he or she repented first (Ibn Ghannam, 1949, 1:176). True worship rested on a mixture of love, hope, and fear directed solely at God – and no one and nothing else (al-Rumi et al., eds, 1978, *'Aqida*, 1:383). Only the Prophet was the model to be followed in everything he believed, said, and did. Though a valid intercessor, even he should not become the object of worship or of a cult (Laoust, 1939, 519–20).

In its dual facet, *tawhid* was the first duty of every Muslim. Understanding and practising it was not the preserve of the elite. Every Muslim had to find out and learn about *tawhid*, regardless of gender, social standing, or level of education (Ibn Ghannam, 1949, 1:147). The religiously educated had the same duty to study it and its antithesis, ignorance, as the common person (ibid.). Only a person who knew ignorance, and could recognize it around him or her, would know the truth and the Qur'an (ibid., 1:105).

As embodied in the *shahada*, *tawhid* was more important than the other pillars of the faith (the five daily prayers, alms, fasting in Ramadan, and the pilgrimage) (Rida, ed., 1999, 27). Observance of those duties availed the Muslim nothing without *tawhid* and anyone who disavowed it or deviated from it was an infidel. Someone dedicated to it (i.e. a *muwahhid*) was guaranteed heaven, just as someone committed to polytheism would enter the fire, however personally pious (Ibn Qasim, ed., 1996–9, 2:32). A neutral stance on *tawhid* was impermissible. There was no third way. "What is there beyond the truth but error?" Ibn 'Abd al-Wahhab demanded to know (al-Rumi et al., eds, 1978, *RS*, 183).

As the antithesis of ignorance, associationism, and unbelief, *tawhid* for Ibn 'Abd al-Wahhab had universal application and transcended issues of narrow difference between the law schools. These had become not merely a specialist area of study and expertise but, to his critical eye, the essence of religious knowledge instead of *tawhid*. In a statement that must have infuriated clerical counterparts, he once declared that only a madman would speak of unity in religion; those hostile to the true knowledge imparted by God (i.e. *tawhid*) were the ones who had become experts in jurisprudence and clerics. They concentrated on divisive petty rules and distinctions and ignored the widespread practice of polytheism all around them (Rida, ed., 1999, 182–3).

For Ibn 'Abd al-Wahhab the Oneness of God was the overriding concept that would unify Muslims around the core of the faith, purged of local variations and accretions, and appeal to Sunnis whatever their affiliations and schools of law. There could be no differences or plurality of view about *tawhid*, which lay at the very heart of Islam.

As we have seen, critics working to discredit Ibn 'Abd al-Wahhab alleged that, despite lacking the most basic qualifications, he claimed to exercise *ijtihad*. Only a practitioner of this (*mujtahid*) was entitled to rely directly on the Qur'an and the *Sunna* instead of on books written within the four schools. On a traditional view, the criteria for this exceptional status were so demanding that no Sunni scholar had fulfilled them for many centuries.

An exasperated Ibn 'Abd al-Wahhab insisted that *ijtihad* applied to jurisprudence. It had no relevance to the simple overriding theological concept of God's Oneness. Even a stupid common person could interpret the Qur'an. The assumption that only an absolute *mujtahid* could know and interpret it and the *Sunna* was the work of the devil (Rida, ed., 1999, 184; Ibn Ghannam, 1949, 1:211). Sinlessness lay in following the Qur'an, not clerics. The Qur'an guarded against error and was as applicable in the twelfth Islamic century, and into the future, as it had been in the first century and thereafter (ibid., 1:210, 212).

TAWHID IN ACTION

Ibn 'Abd al-Wahhab stressed that for the Muslim simple knowledge of the Oneness of God was not enough. Even if accompanied by renunciation of polytheism, it did not guarantee entry into heaven (Ibn Qasim, ed., 1996–9, 1:171). There had to be action on *tawhid*. He insisted:

> There is no dispute that *tawhid* must be in the heart, on the tongue and by deed. If there is any deficiency in this, a man is no Muslim. If he knows *tawhid* and does not act on it, he is an unbeliever (*kafir*) and disobedient [to God], like the Pharaoh, Devil and such like. Many of the people make this mistake, saying this is the truth and we understand and witness it as such but cannot practise it because the people of our town allow only those who agree with them, and other such excuses ... Practising *tawhid* is an outward activity, and he who does not understand and believe it in his heart is a hypocrite worse than an outright infidel.
>
> (Rida, ed., 1999, 120–1)

Private piety was insufficient. A Muslim had not only to recognize and practise *tawhid* in his or her own personal life and activities but to demonstrate adherence in the public space by objecting to the polytheism of others (Ibn Ghannam, 1949, 1:96, 139). The battle with unbelief was not abstract or distant (ibid., 1:118). Unbelief was real and all around. One had to be able to recognize it to denounce and contest it. The true believer could not stand aside and absolve him- or herself of the responsibility to interfere by saying that the people's condition was known to God and it was for Him to resolve (ibid., 1:181). Every Muslim had to be both activist and interventionist.

Readiness publicly to uphold *tawhid* in action demanded moral and physical bravery. Ibn 'Abd al-Wahhab set a personal example of physical fearlessness in refusing to be muzzled in Basra and Huraymila. He demonstrated moral courage in al-'Uyayna when he took personal charge of destroying the tomb and mosque at al-Jubayla, defying popular hostility and the inevitable accusation that he was belittling Companions of the Prophet.

Ibn 'Abd al-Wahhab was clear that the duty to practise and enforce *tawhid* overrode ties of country, tribe, or family, just as awe of God had to outweigh fear of other people (ibid., 1:106). Concern about losing worldly status, wealth, family, or friends could not justify refusal to practise or implement *tawhid* (Rida, ed., 1999, 121). The Wahhabi was not to be deflected by tribal pressures or worldly considerations. His relationships with others were to be determined by his duties as a believer. He was to cut contact with unbelievers and polytheists, even if that meant disowning his own father, brothers, or children (Ibn Ghannam, 1949, 1:177; Rida, ed., 1999, 159). Ibn 'Abd al-Wahhab himself broke openly with his brother and more distant relatives once he had performed his filial duty by suspending his campaign in Huraymila until his disapproving father died.

Ibn 'Abd al-Wahhab recognized human love for property and children as natural but considered it permissible only if did not lead to disobedience to God or serious sin (al-Rumi et al., eds, 1978, *'Aqida*, 1:382). The true Muslim should love his fellow believers in *tawhid* and treat them as brothers, even if geographically distant (Ibn Ghannam, 1949, 1:177). Shared belief and action were the exclusive basis of loyalty under God's banner. Family, home, tribal section, and property were all rivals to God and might seduce the believer from true Islam. He had to cut his link with all but God (Rida, ed., 1928, 4:34–5), and pursue the truth wherever it took him.

FRIENDS, ENEMIES, AND THE FIFTH COLUMN

Underlying this stance was the core precept of friendly association with believers and disassociation from unbelievers (known as *al-wala' wa-al-bara'*). Sometimes he made this doctrine of loyalty one of the three fundamentals of true religion, with the two basic forms of *tawhid* (Rida, ed., 1928, 1:4). It determined his approach to excommunicating unbelievers (*takfir*) and emigration (*hijra*), especially once he moved from the language of disengaging from polytheists to that of enmity toward them, wherever they were. He pronounced: "a person's Islam is not sound even if he practises *tawhid* of God and deserts polytheism unless he is hostile to polytheists and declares to them his hostility and hatred" (Rida, ed., 1999, 140). A Muslim who loved Islam was not a proper believer if he drew no distinction between friends and enemies. There could be no two valid confessions in the same religion (al-Rumi et al., eds, 1978, *RS*, 183).

Behind this approach, which bred a potentially isolationist and insular outlook, was the belief that society was composed of antithetical forces of true Muslims ranged against polytheists. Just as Wahhabis of both sexes should and would ally with one another (Rida, ed., 1928, 4:37), so would polytheists. But there was a third group which would also act collectively: the hypocrites (Ibn Sihman, ed., 1925/6, 33). They presented themselves as believers but did not believe inwardly and were guilty of fundamental hypocrisy beyond minor acts of lying or betrayal of the community (Rida, ed., 1928, 4:13). They were enemies of God and His Prophet and represented a potential fifth column. They sided with the Wahhabis from opportunism, not conviction. The Wahhabis faced an ever-present risk that, when the movement came under heavy pressure from opponents, such elements would betray it. They did so in the crisis of 1753 when many settlements reneged on proclaimed Wahhabi allegiance.

Ibn 'Abd al-Wahhab's wariness of the danger from a fifth column accounts for the strong antipathy in his writings to those who gave alms, prayed, fasted, waged *jihad*, and appeared to believe and implement *tawhid*, yet whose adherence to the Wahhabi cause was driven by worldly motives, such as commerce, desire for status, or social ties (al-Rumi et al., eds, 1978, *RS*, 96). These people resiled from allegiance when it suited their interests. Once their hypocrisy was unmasked they became apostates and belonged in a lower place in hell even than outright unbelievers, whom they exceeded in evil (Rida, ed., 1928, 4:12; Rida, ed., 1999, 120–1).

The threat from hypocrites was less one of individual betrayal than of a collective repudiation of allegiance. Hypocrites of both sexes would stick together as much as did believers or polytheists (Ibn Sihman, ed., 1925/6, 33). It was vital to distinguish the true supporter from the hypocrite (Ibn Ghannam, 1949, 1:102) and to purge the vanguard community of treacherous sympathizers before confronting outright Muslim opponents. The closest enemy was the most dangerous, and *jihad* against the hypocrites at a time when Islam was rarely practised properly was the finest form of *jihad* (ibid., 1:159).

A COMMUNITY APART

The community of true believers stood at the center of Ibn 'Abd al-Wahhab's vision. His version of it implied egalitarianism among believers. Whoever acted in line with Wahhabi beliefs was a brother (or sister) Muslim. This emphasis on religious loyalty and equality of believers overriding tribal allegiances and hierarchies was highly contentious in a deeply traditional society. Whether townspeople or pastoralists, local Najdis believed in tribal castes, genealogies, communitarian values, reciprocal obligations, and the consensus of kinsmen, even if constant migration had weakened tribal structures in southern Najd. For the Wahhabis to go further and demand not just dissociation from polytheists among close family (and a ban on marriage to female polytheists) but hostility to them was a direct challenge to existing bonds of social cohesion based on family solidarity and hierarchies.

In substituting loyalty to *tawhid* and fellow Wahhabis, whatever their background, tribe, or status, as the determining duty and virtue, and in demanding hostility to enemies of the Wahhabi community, Ibn 'Abd al-Wahhab aimed to tighten the bonds of allegiance among Wahhabis and distance them from the rest of the Sunni community. Wahhabis were to be distinctive, a group apart. This politically and socially radical stance generated many of the charges of sectarianism. It also caused persistent controversy and anxiety among those subject to Wahhabi proselytizing and campaigning.

5

IDEOLOGUE OF STRUGGLE

Ibn 'Abd al-Wahhab adopted *tawhid* as the theological redoubt of true faith. He encircled this with ideological ramparts, concepts designed to protect believers from the pernicious influence of idolaters and the Shi'a, exclude infidels and apostates, and provide a launchpad for *jihad*. This chapter considers these concepts, which served as ideological drivers for Wahhabi campaigning and as justification for Saudi expansionism.

EXCOMMUNICATION (*TAKFIR*)

Ibn 'Abd al-Wahhab's refusal to accept pluralism of belief or compromise, coupled with relentless focus on the nature and definition of polytheism, reflected a Manichean – black or white – approach that runs like a thread through his writings. These concentrate on how to distinguish between *tawhid* and unbelief (*kufr*), between true Muslims and those who might nominally be Muslims but had corrupted the faith. As critics observed, he drew these lines with such remorseless rigor that he placed most Muslims of his era on the wrong side (Sulayman ibn 'Abd al-Wahhab, 2005, 13). They said he designated as an unbeliever anyone who disagreed with him, did not follow him, or was beyond his control (Ibn Ghannam, 1949, 1:112, 153).

Ibn 'Abd al-Wahhab's response to this charge could be glib: he was designating as infidels not Muslims but polytheists (ibid., 1:147). His starting point was that apostates in Islamic law could not be only those who converted from Islam to Judaism, Christianity, or Zoroastrianism.

They had to include those who did not believe in *tawhid* or practise it (ibid., 1:142–3). A simple claim to belong to the Islamic community, declaration of the *shahada*, or performance of the five pillars of Islam could not disqualify someone from being an apostate (*murtadd*). Otherwise worship of idols that did not involve complete renunciation of Islam would remain unpunished. What too of hypocrites who performed their duties, including *jihad*, yet did not believe? Anyone claiming to Islam would be a Muslim, unless he rejected Islam in its entirety or practised another religion. Only someone claiming to belong to another religious community would be an unbeliever. Such a conclusion would be "a great scandal" (al-Rumi et al., eds, 1978, *'Aqida*, 1:307, 309).

Early opponents, in some cases sympathetic to Ibn 'Abd al-Wahhab's reformist goal but not his doctrinal methodology, said he was preaching the true religion except for his insistence on excommunication (*takfir*) and *jihad* (Ibn Ghannam, 1949, 1:150; al-Rumi et al., eds, 1978, *RS*, 183, 272). They considered commission of the more heinous forms of polytheism (known as greater *shirk*) or unbelief did not justify *takfir* or charges of apostasy. Nor did they result in designation of territory as under infidel control and so subject to *jihad* (known in Islamic law as "the territory of war," *dar al-harb*) (Sulayman ibn 'Abd al-Wahhab, 2005, 12–13). In their view there had to be the clearest proof before *takfir* of a Muslim. It exposed him or her in this world to automatic legal penalties, including a loss of all legal rights that legitimized his or her killing. The body was not then to be washed, prayed over, or buried among Muslims. His or her fate in the next world was eternal hellfire, worse even than that prescribed for Jews or Christians (al-Rumi et al., eds, 1978, *'Aqida*, 1:328).

Contemporary critics argued that the prevailing religious situation was no worse than it had been over the previous 700 years. They wondered what Wahhabi beliefs signified for the status of previous generations of Muslims. Were they all now to be classified as unbelievers and apostates (Sulayman ibn 'Abd al-Wahhab, 2005, 58)? Did Wahhabi *takfir* project back into the past, meaning that the fathers and ancestors of contemporary Najdis had died in a state of unbelief? Was Ibn 'Abd al-Wahhab annulling existing marriages entered into in a state of ignorance (Ibn Ghannam, 1949, 1:153)? Or invalidating previous pilgrimages?

This critique, based on a long tradition of tolerance and fear of the ineluctable legal, theological, and political consequences of *takfir*, viewed it as a weapon of division, fragmentation, and oppression. A millennium of religious experience had shown that, if deployed freely by individual clerics such as Ibn 'Abd al-Wahhab, it could destroy any semblance of political unity or social cohesion. Unsurprisingly he dismissed this argument as the very essence of unbelief. How could Muslims who loved the truth not grasp that *takfir* and *jihad* could not be detached from *tawhid* but were inextricably tied to it (al-Rumi et al., eds, 1978, *RS*, 183)?

Ibn 'Abd al-Wahhab acknowledged certain safeguards for *takfir* given its consequences. Accusations based on hearsay or supposition could not support a verdict of unbelief (Ibn Ghannam, 1949, 1:107). If an unbeliever were found guilty of worshiping other than God, he had a chance to repent. Only if he refused was he to be killed (ibid., 1:117). Ibn 'Abd al-Wahhab also allowed the excuse of outright duress provided the believer's faith remained unshaken. Although he did not spell out the requirements for this, he implied direct physical threat to the person concerned, not just fear of impact on home, family, tribe or property (Rida, ed., 1999, 121). A broad notion of precautionary dissimulation (*taqiyya*) was not to undermine his demand for loyalty to the faith. This license for hypocrisy was the hallmark of the hated Shi'a, whose doctrine of *taqiyya* made many Sunnis suspect their motives and sincerity.

Ibn 'Abd al-Wahhab believed it legitimate in Islamic law to proclaim the unbelief of both specific individuals and whole communities. With specific, directed excommunication, the individual targeted had to have had true Islam explained to him through advice (*nasiha*) or the medium of preachers. In the case of those who did not, or could not, know better, any verdict of *takfir* had to be suspended until it was clear they had been presented with Qur'anic proof, even if they did not understand it. If the Qur'an had reached them and they had no excuse for disregarding it, they were infidels unless judged sinners or guilty of stubborn disobedience (al-Rumi et al., eds, 1978, *'Aqida*, 1:289; Ibn Ghannam, 1949, 1:168, 182–3).

This view that the Qur'an constituted proof, and that anyone the Qur'an had reached had been presented with the proof, rested on the contention that the Qur'an was not hard to understand and was patently categoric in banning the association of others with God (ibid., 1:182). Anti-Wahhabis disputed this. Some critics, including brother Sulayman, insisted the presentation of proof be clear, direct, and personal from a qualified teacher, not assumed from a widely addressed letter of advice or mere availability of the Qur'an. For a verdict of *kufr* the target had to understand what was at stake. Even if he did and still did not conform, he was exonerated if subject to duress from an opponent or understandable confusions or doubts (Sulayman ibn 'Abd al-Wahhab, 2005, 18, 38, 41, 49).

After Ibn 'Abd al-Wahhab's death the Wahhabi position started to ease. It had featured the unforgiving requirement that proof should have been presented directly or indirectly, whether understood or not. It became less hard-line: there had to be a cleric or proselytizer available to explain the Qur'anic precepts clearly, even if the target still did not understand (Rida, ed., 1928, 1:248). Later Wahhabi clerics made understanding a requirement. For Ibn 'Abd al-Wahhab that was an unacceptable let-out.

Later too there was a doctrinal shift in relation to mass or blanket *takfir*, which applied to everyone in an area or settlement, learned and ignorant together, and whether or not presented with proof. Ibn 'Abd al-Wahhab insisted he and his followers did not pronounce *takfir* of people indiscriminately (Ibn Ghannam, 1949, 1:180). But the early Wahhabis did on occasion pronounce *takfir* of whole settlements. This triggered an obligation on Wahhabis not just to boycott them but to wage *jihad* against them. Recognition that within a designated settlement there might be pious people whose religion could not be faulted led Ibn 'Abd al-Wahhab's successors to hold that mass *takfir* did not mean everyone was necessarily a *kafir* (Rida, ed., 1928, 1:44). They even suggested it might be better to avoid a definitive ruling rather than engage in blanket *takfir* (Ibn Qasim, ed., 1996–9, 9:254).

These doctrinal modifications underline the danger when analysing Wahhabi teachings of borrowing freely from Wahhabi writings without considering how doctrines and the way they were applied changed over the movement's career, including in the eight decades of the First Saudi State. The broad outlines of the Wahhabi controversy may have remained static over centuries. But Wahhabi thinking shifted subtly even before the end of the First Saudi State, especially once Saudi forces moved beyond Najd into regions with more mixed populations.

SECONDARY *TAKFIR* AND EMIGRATION (*HIJRA*)

Within a settlement confronted by the advance of Wahhabism, who fell subject to *takfir*? In the first instance, those who opposed *tawhid*, approved of polytheistic practices (as defined by the Wahhabis), or endorsed its practitioners (Ibn Ghannam, 1949, 1:107–8). Believers in *tawhid* who renounced idolatry and disliked polytheists, but were based in towns where people were explicitly hostile to *tawhid*, could be vulnerable. If they argued that they could not desert their home towns and ended up fighting the Wahhabis alongside fellow townspeople, they too were categorized as unbelievers (al-Rumi et al., eds, 1978, *RS*, 272–3; see Rida, ed., 1999, 178). This ruling applied especially to those rulers who sympathized with Wahhabism but took an anti-Wahhabi line out of fear of popular rebellion (or of being subordinated to or sidelined by the Al Sa'ud) (Ibn Ghannam, 1949, 1:109–10).

Siding with anti-Wahhabis, which might entail *takfir* of Wahhabis, waging *jihad* against them, or funding anti-Wahhabi activity, constituted unbelief for the Wahhabis. This was so whether or not the individual personally observed *tawhid* or was guilty of idolatry (Ibn Ghannam, 1949, 1:109, 180). Fear of the reactions of family, neighbors, or fellow townsfolk conferred no exemption. Still less did material motivation like a desire to trade, make a living, or preserve wealth or status (al-Rumi et al., eds, 1978, *'Aqida*, 1:297–8). Unbelief might be driven by the very best of religious motives yet remain unbelief (Ibn Ghannam, 1949, 1:179).

The above would suggest that someone who believed in *tawhid*, did not commit polytheism himself or herself, associated with polytheists but did not assist them in any way against the Wahhabis, and did not denounce or combat unbelief, was innocent of unbelief. However, such a person would have occupied a no man's land between Wahhabis and polytheists, an unacceptable outcome for Ibn 'Abd al-Wahhab. He wanted to compel not just every cleric but every individual to take sides. At times he insisted he did not pronounce *takfir* on the basis solely of friendly association with polytheists (ibid., 1:108). At others he described such association as rank unbelief (ibid., 1:142). In one broad statement to a supporter he demanded that a true Muslim be free of both polytheism and polytheists (al-Rumi et al., eds, 1978, *RS*, 60). He had to be openly hostile to polytheists and proclaim his hatred of them (al-Rumi et al., eds, 1978, *'Aqida*, 1:355).

With such pronouncements on record it is small wonder Ibn 'Abd al-Wahhab's denials of Wahhabi *takfir* on the basis of association did not convince opponents. They complained that he defined too tightly who was a Muslim. Following his ideological mentor Ibn Taymiyya, he also insisted that anyone who did not pronounce *takfir* of an infidel was himself one, even if he had otherwise done nothing wrong (Sulayman ibn 'Abd al-Wahhab, 2005, 12–13, 45, 58). Such secondary *takfir* (my phrase, not a Wahhabi term) ensured the sharp split in society that Ibn 'Abd al-Wahhab wanted. He obfuscated his position at times yet wielded this weapon of secondary *takfir* to compel support for the Wahhabis and to segregate them from their enemies.

Secondary *takfir* tied into the potentially isolationist concept of emigration (*hijra*). In Islam this has both a physical aspect and a metaphorical dimension. Harking back to the Prophet's withdrawal from godless Mecca to Medina, emigration traditionally represents a physical move to the land of Islam (*dar al-Islam*) from territory where unbelief predominates (*dar al-kufr* or *dar al-harb*). Although some Islamic thinkers had developed the idea of an intermediate, neutral territory, the early Wahhabis ruled out any such half-way status (Ibn Qasim, ed., 1996–9, 9:248).

Physical emigration featured early in the Wahhabi story when Ibn 'Abd al-Wahhab created a haven in al-Dir'iyya. His followers left al-'Uyayna to join him, leaving behind their local positions, property, and wider families. This caused physical hardship because of the sudden strain on al-Dir'iyya's limited resources. Ibn 'Abd al-Wahhab laid on welfare arrangements to ensure that families which had migrated to al-Dir'iyya without money did not go hungry or have to beg, until conditions improved (Ibn Ghannam, 1949, 1:170; Ibn Bishr, 1982–3, 1:43).

The parallels in language Wahhabis drew with the first years of Islam prompted opponents to warn against the arrogance of the analogy (Sulayman ibn 'Abd al-Wahhab, 2005, 25). They also claimed he required Wahhabis to leave their home towns to join him even when they were able to observe *tawhid* publicly there (Ibn Ghannam, 1949, 1:180). Ibn 'Abd al-Wahhab persistently denied this. Opponents claimed he required anyone who could not designate his town's inhabitants as infidels to emigrate from the land of unbelief, even if that included the Holy Places themselves (Sulayman ibn 'Abd al-Wahhab, 2005, 13).

Ibn 'Abd al-Wahhab's starting point was his desire for true Muslims to practise their religion wherever they were (al-Rumi et al., eds, 1978, *RS*, 58). He feared that life in a town where polytheism prevailed would involve association with polytheists and distance from true Muslims. This would lead a Muslim into polytheism not through duress but gradually through fear or persuasion, or thanks to worldly reasons, including love of family, possessions, or home (Ibn Ghannam, 1949, 1:166).

He insisted that a Muslim able to manifest or proclaim his religion was allowed to remain beyond Wahhabi territory. He did not define what he meant by "manifest" or "proclaim". That said, only if these terms involved outright *takfir* of local polytheists could this square with Wahhabi secondary *takfir* of those who associated with polytheists and yet did not pronounce *takfir* of them. Here again Wahhabi doctrine became more nuanced once Ibn 'Abd al-Wahhab's sons headed the religious establishment (see Rida, ed., 1928, 1:39–40).

The prudent Wahhabi resident of a hostile settlement where he could not risk proclaiming *takfir* of anti-Wahhabis would have been well advised to leave for Wahhabi-held territory, unless he could exploit a narrowly defined exemption based on duress or physical disability. Otherwise he risked Wahhabi excommunication involving death and seizure of property.

However, any Wahhabi ruling probably depended on the specific circumstances of the case and the wider demands of the Wahhabi movement at the time. When the Saudis were advancing in a district, they would hardly have benefited from local Wahhabis withdrawing from settlements that the Saudis aimed to win over. By contrast, a broad application of *hijra* suited a defensive phase for the Wahhabis when they were consolidating or retreating. Significantly, as warfare spread across Najd in the mid-eighteenth century, anti-Saudi rulers showed growing reluctance to let leading pro-Wahhabis in their towns depart for al-Dir'iyya, while the Saudis took increasingly to expelling anti-Wahhabis from towns they captured.

When the Saudis were expanding, the concept of *hijra* gave compelling encouragement to local Wahhabis in neutral or even hostile settlements to parade their version of Islam. Better to show hostility to polytheists among fellow townsmen than to submit to the majority's will. For they knew they would be called to account on Saudi conquest. Yet there must have been cases too where Saudi interests required Wahhabis to preserve the element of subversive clandestinity that characterized the movement before 1744. Here the Saudi cause would not have been served by either emigration or overt protestation of Wahhabi loyalties or doctrine, whatever Wahhabi clerics prescribed.

Hijra could also form the conceptual justification for an aggressive commercial or trading boycott of areas controlled by unbelieving rulers. Ibn 'Abd al-Wahhab harbored general distaste for worldly considerations and the individual's desire for reward in this world as opposed to the next. He had a prejudice against commercial motives and readily dismissed the trader's argument for dealing with polytheists. To his mind a small monetary profit did not outweigh the penalty for apostasy of eternal fire (Ibn Ghannam, 1949, 1:170).

Ibn 'Abd al-Wahhab never devoted as much doctrinal attention to the parameters and implications of *hijra* as did his young grandson, the hard-line ideologue Sulayman, son of 'Abd Allah. Sulayman was confronted by Egypt's steadily advancing military machine in the final years of the First Saudi State. He responded by championing the concept of *hijra*. He set out detailed rules to cover commercial links between Wahhabis and those beyond Saudi territory. Renowned for both his talent and his intransigence, he was singled out for execution by Ibrahim Pasha, the Egyptian commander, who showed contempt for Wahhabi mores by having music played to Sulayman first (Ibn Bishr, 1982–3, 1:424).

As well as physical emigration, *hijra* in Islam also signifies metaphorical transfer from tribal bonds and loyalties based on descent to membership of the Islamic community with its accompanying commitments and responsibilities. In Wahhabi doctrine submission to God and loyalty to fellow believers were the determining allegiances in the believer's life. Together with obedience to the Saudi guarantors of the regime of godliness, these were the only valid drivers for action. The supreme expression of submission to God and of communal solidarity in action was *jihad*. There could be no true religion without it. It was the required response not just to unbelief but to renunciation or non-performance of any of the key elements of Islam (Ibn Qasim, ed., 1996–9, 9:246–7).

JIHAD

Ibn 'Abd al-Wahhab acknowledged that force was integral to *tawhid* and required "the unsheathing of the sword" (al-Rumi et al., eds, 1978, *'Aqida*, 1:284). This was "so that there should cease to be civil strife (*fitna*) and all religion should belong to God" (Q. viii:39). If by consensus death was the punishment for contesting one of the bases of Islam, how could it not be the penalty for repudiating *tawhid*, which was the very foundation of the religion (Rida, ed., 1999, 117)? If God ordered *jihad* by word and deed against unbelievers and hypocrites, the believer had no choice but to wage it (Ibn Ghannam, 1949, 1:189).

The obligation to wage *jihad* was absolute and its conduct had to have the right motive (i.e. not purely a desire for booty) (ibid., 1:159, 178). Ibn 'Abd al-Wahhab was scathing about those who wavered or hung back. He criticized the people of one settlement who were supposed to have sided with the Saudis but declined to campaign against a neighboring town. He accused them pungently of "preferring the ephemeral to the eternal, and selling pearls for dung and goodness for evil" (al-Rumi et al., eds, 1978, *RS*, 293).

In traditional Hanbali legal scholarship to which Ibn 'Abd al-Wahhab subscribed, the declaration of *jihad* against non-Muslims had to be preceded by a summons to the enemy to convert unless they were already familiar with the message (al-Rumi et al., eds, 1978, *Fiqh*, 1:372). The Wahhabis followed this precept with bedouin ignorant of the Qur'an and *Sunna*. They required the Wahhabi message to have reached the nomads through preachers and propagators before they could be said to have rejected the summons. But that precondition did not apply to deviant fellow Muslims already familiar with the Qur'an and *Sunna*, nor to bedouin who had received the summons years before and ignored it (Ibn Qasim, ed., 1996–9, 9:245). Once the Wahhabi campaign had been running for some years, Ibn 'Abd al-Wahhab probably regarded every Najdi as on notice of the Qur'anic proofs, whether or not he or she accepted them.

Ibn 'Abd al-Wahhab claimed the Wahhabis were the victims of aggressive *jihad*, not its initiators, and that his enemies were the first ones to pronounce *takfir* (al-Rumi et al., eds, 1978, *RS*, 158). In fact he took the first step by excommunicating local holy men and their followers and refusing to distinguish between holy men, saints, and Sufis in his condemnations. This led to *takfir* of the Wahhabis by local and regional opponents and then, in the Wahhabi narrative, to their persecution by local rulers and clerics. At this point the Wahhabis' *jihad* could properly be classified as defensive. Yet it was a conflict precipitated by Ibn 'Abd al-Wahhab's own ideology and actions. His doctrines and ambitions were destined, even intended, to turn the struggle between Wahhabis and their opponents into violent confrontation, for all that tactically he did not welcome its timing (Crawford, 2011, 159–60). Once in al-Dir'iyya, having summoned neighboring towns to convert and endured ridicule in response, he is alleged by Ibn Bishr to have declared offensive *jihad* (Ibn Bishr, 1982–3, 1:45–6, 48).

Traditional Islamic jurisprudence, including in Hanbalism, lays down that it is for the ruler, whether tyrannical or just, to declare offensive *jihad*. For this imposes a collective duty on the community.

By contrast defensive *jihad* entails individual obligations. It is therefore odd that by this account it was the *shaykh*, not the Saudi ruler, who ordered the Wahhabi community to wage *jihad*. This is all the more striking because the *jihad* lasted the lifetime of the First Saudi State. It defined its territorial, financial and institutional development. Since Saudi domains acknowledged no territorial frontiers and Wahhabism no boundary to the regime of godliness, the community embarked on war that could end only in complete victory or annihilation.

This was the inexorable outcome of Ibn 'Abd al-Wahhab's doctrines. They were calculated to split the Islamic community and precipitate a struggle between Wahhabis and anti-Wahhabis. The dogma of *tawhid* defined the cause; the doctrine of association with believers and disassociation from unbelievers secured loyalty; the concepts of primary and secondary *takfir* singled out the enemy; emigration (*hijra*) helped marshal the forces; and *jihad* was the necessary, if violent, expedient for achieving God's will.

That the Saudi state was destroyed and the Wahhabi movement nearly extinguished as a result of pursuing these doctrines was a bewildering outcome for Wahhabis. It tormented generations of clerics and cast a long shadow over the next century of Saudi history. Before reviewing this outcome, we should look at the primary targets for Ibn 'Abd al-Wahhab's campaign of preaching, *takfir* and *jihad*, his approach to governance, and the connection between Wahhabism and Saudi state formation.

6

SCOURGE OF POLYTHEISTS

The last two chapters outlined the concepts that determined Ibn 'Abd al-Wahhab's world view, with *tawhid*, the Oneness of God, at its center. For him Muslims could not know and appreciate this unless they had known its antithesis, ignorance (Ibn Ghannam, 1949, 1:105). This meant recognizing the main forces of irreligion in society: in his eyes, Sunni clerical opponents, nomads, Sufis, and Shi'a. Over its first two centuries these were Wahhabism's main enemies before strains within the movement, blended with other Islamist beliefs, threatened its integrity.

SUNNI CLERICAL OPPONENTS

Ibn 'Abd al-Wahhab held clerics accountable for the sorry state of contemporary Islam (ibid., 1:95–7). In confronting them he faced a dilemma. He challenged their authority and advocated an alternative basis of religious truth. Yet he had to recognize the confidence that ill-educated, largely illiterate communities had in them, a trust that was rooted in tradition, family ties, and the political and social status quo. If he was to create a popular movement, he had to coopt or subdue some of these alternative poles of authority but without subverting their local standing. This meant striking the right balance between persuasion, cajoling, and outright pressure. This task was complicated by the essentially rejectionist and exclusivist nature of his message.

Attaching the Wahhabi campaign to the political and dynastic cause of the Al Sa'ud brought benefits in a fragmented society. It also increased resistance, injecting a political element into religious and ideological opposition that intensified as Saudi expansionism threatened the interests, as well as the beliefs, of many notables, including clerics. Ibn 'Abd al-Wahhab appreciated clerics would be pressurized by local rulers or prove unable to sway them toward Wahhabism. He still rejected their claims of powerlessness and criticized them for failing to advise rulers properly. He emphasized that they should not kowtow to popular practices or pressure.

One of his refrains was that most contemporary clerics recognized in private that the Wahhabi position on *tawhid* was right because it was so well supported by the Qur'an, even if they themselves practised polytheism, waged or endorsed *jihad* against the Wahhabis, or persecuted them (al-Rumi et al., eds, 1978, *'Aqida*, 1:306). It became an enduring Wahhabi line that recognition of the Wahhabis' rightness only increased opponents' rebellion against God (Rida, ed., 1999, 334). Ibn 'Abd al-Wahhab convinced himself that the Wahhabis would win over most clerics and educated people. They first had to eliminate worldly obstructions and motivations (by definition base in nature). They told interlocutors regularly to consider their eternal salvation, not short-term advantage (Ibn Qasim, ed., 1996–9, 1:283). The *shaykh* warned correspondents implicitly but unmistakably that the Wahhabis would win in the end. And their opponents would suffer (Rida, ed., 1928, 1:6).

Ibn 'Abd al-Wahhab's epistles are undated so we cannot track easily how he handled local clerics. These letters were the main medium for dispensing his advice (*nasiha*), designed to bind in supporters and win over opponents. They were often read out aloud in settlements, triggering discussion and controversy (Ibn Ghannam, 1949, 1:140). As part of his effort with clerics, teachers (*muttawwi'in*), notables, and pupils in both mosque and *majlis*, he tried in the first years, when travel allowed, to stage personal encounters with opposing clerics in the *majlis* to discuss key religious works. He complained that many ducked text-based exchanges and appealed instead to *shaykhs* in the Holy Cities or elsewhere (al-Rumi et al., eds, 1978, *RS*, 273). When he agreed to an anti-Wahhabi rulers' request to discuss the writings of later jurists, he claimed they pulled out and became still more hostile (Ibn Ghannam,

1949, 1:153–4). Later he despatched Wahhabi clerics to pursue formal disputations with regional counterparts. He and his followers often misjudged the outcomes. Belief in their own rightness and righteousness often seemed to blind them to the reactions of others.

Ibn 'Abd al-Wahhab's bitterest early Najdi opponents were Sulayman ibn Suhaym (d. 1767) (and his father Muhammad) of Riyadh, 'Abd Allah al-Muways (d. 1761/2) of Harma, and his own brother Sulayman (d. 1794), all Hanbalis. All three were associated with anti-Saudi forces and enlisted support from regional anti-Wahhabis. In al-Ahsa these included Hanbali Muhammad ibn 'Afaliq (d. 1750), Shafi'i 'Abd Allah ibn 'Abd al-Latif (d. 1751/2), and Maliki 'Isa ibn 'Abd al-Rahman ibn Mutlaq (d. 1784), among the older generation. Younger critics there included another relative of Ibn 'Abd al-Wahhab, the highly influential Hanbali Muhammad ibn Fayruz (d. 1801/2). Other vocal regional opponents included the Shafi'i Ahmad ibn 'Ali al-Qabbani in Basra, the Meccan clerics from all the schools who condemned him in 1743, and later Shafi'is Muhammad ibn Sulayman al-Kurdi of Medina (d. 1780) and 'Alawi al-Haddad of the Hadramawt.

We await a detailed analysis of anti-Wahhabi clerics in central Arabia and their motivations in the early decades. They seem to have been driven variously by one or a combination of theological or ideological dislike of Wahhabi doctrines; Sufi affiliations; fear of popular reactions; attachment to anti-Saudi rulers; fear of the divisive impact of Wahhabism's religious, political, and social radicalism on vulnerable or hybrid societies; and worries about their own status or incomes.

Ibn 'Abd al-Wahhab's refusal to accept compromise between the antithetical forces of *tawhid* and *shirk* and their proponents meant he disallowed middle ground. As we have seen, he demanded to know what could lie beyond the truth but error (e.g. Ibn Ghannam, 1949, 1:53). Two confessions could not exist within one religion (al-Rumi et al., eds, 1978, *RS*, 183). Clerics were either for or against him. They could not preserve neutrality or refuse to commit themselves in the ideological contest. The issue was too momentous for such detachment (Ibn Ghannam, 1949, 1:172). Pursuing this approach he won over some clerics but drove others inexorably into open opposition. Pragmatic at times, he would not compromise on *tawhid*.

Opposing Najdi clerics appear rarely to have been targeted systematically by either the Wahhabis or their enemies. Despite reciprocal *takfir* that exposed leading proponents to murder or plunder, each side seems generally to have observed a convention respecting the status of clerics. This did not bestow complete immunity from attack or retaliation. There were some egregious examples of Wahhabi clerics suffering summary execution in Najd. Likewise some anti-Wahhabi clerics were killed there.

Despite their prominence in the ideological conflict, most clerics survived the fall of their home towns to opponents. Whether saved by expulsion, safe conduct, or flight, they remained free to resume the struggle from fresh pulpits. These became harder for anti-Wahhabis to find as the Saudi noose tightened around the districts of al-Washm, Sudayr, and al-Qasim. Critics then had to choose between escaping to al-Ahsa, Basra, al-Zubayr, al-Zubara, or the Holy Cities, or submitting to the Wahhabis.

Appreciating the need to reconcile and accommodate some of them, Ibn 'Abd al-Wahhab forgave certain local religious critics, even his brother Sulayman, though he did not let them impose conditions. Nor would he accept any kind of fudged position by opponents once their cause started to fail (Rida, ed., 1928, 1:5). Many of those who submitted were forced to reside in al-Dir'iyya. This was for reindoctrination, to allow the Saudis to keep a close eye on them, and to guarantee good conduct in their communities, reflecting a growing Saudi practice of holding opponents hostage in comfortable conditions in the Saudi capital.

THE BEDOUIN

Ibn 'Abd al-Wahhab advocated uniform enforcement of the Wahhabi religious regime across both nomadic and settled populations, and those in transition from one to the other; the replacement of tribal loyalties among all these populations by allegiance to *tawhid* and the Wahhabi community; and the substitution of *zakat* for illegal imposts. Such a program of action was bound to be contentious in the conservative communities across Najd.

This was a society where the balances within settlements, and between desert and sown, were delicately poised and fragile. Clerics were traditionally neutral repositors of learning, mediators and upholders of the status quo, not instigators of religious and social change. The fear of Ibn 'Abd al-Wahhab's critics that he would sharpen discord within and between settlements was borne out by events. His religious campaign caused decades of conflict in Najd and beyond that affected all categories of the population.

Ibn 'Abd al-Wahhab made clear his low opinion of contemporary Najdis. He viewed most of them as ignorant deviationists. They relied on customary law and practice, not the *shari'a*. They drew their smattering of religion from their forefathers and handed traditional beliefs and practices down the generations. A ten-year-old boy could be taught the words for prayer and have only that much religion until the day he died (Rida, ed., 1928, 1:2–3).

The bedouin bore the brunt of Ibn 'Abd al-Wahhab's opprobrium as the epitome of ignorance. This dismayed critics sensitive to the vulnerability of the small towns and villages of central Najd, and their distended lines of communication, to bedouin depredations. They worried that Ibn 'Abd al-Wahhab's aggressive stance toward tribal or customary law would endanger the delicate relationship between settled and nomadic. They dismissed the argument that only unification of communities around *tawhid* could resolve the chronic political instability of Najd and reduce the exposure of settlements to bedouin pressure.

Against this background there is sharp irony in the persistent image, recycled even today by leading commentators, of Wahhabism as a desert movement empowered by the tribal Al Sa'ud. In a classic misreading of Wahhabism, Abou El Fadl declares: "Wahhabis have always equated the austere cultural practices of Bedouin life with the one and only true Islam" (Abou El Fadl, 2007, 47).

The movement was a phenomenon of the small towns and settlements of Najd, not the desert. The greatest asset of the Al Sa'ud was not their tribal lineage or power (they lacked both) but their enduring talent for balancing relationships and interests, and for coalition-building. Originally a small clan, they owed their influence to property holdings, management of agriculture, and trade. It was precisely their detribalized, settled nature that helped make them an effective instrument for driving a campaign that challenged the bedouin lifestyle and primacy of tribal allegiances among the bedouin and some of the settled communities. Conversely, the arrangement with Ibn 'Abd al-Wahhab gave the Al Sa'ud a dynamic basis for generating loyalty beyond the geography of tribal affiliation.

Contemporary observers in the regional metropolises dismissed the Saudis as "Arabs", a term imputing both desert and tribal background and primitive attitudes. The notion, born of ignorance and disdain, of a unified culture in Najd contrasted with the local reality, conveyed by the Wahhabi chroniclers, of ingrained mutual hatred between bedouin and villagers (although in practice there was no sharp dividing line between the two). Ibn Bishr described this antipathy as both longstanding and natural. For Wahhabis the bedouin were as much the antithesis of the settled inhabitants as unbelief was of *tawhid* (Ibn Bishr, 1982–3, 1:270–1).

CUSTOMARY LAW

Ibn 'Abd al-Wahhab's straightforward stance was that true Islam belonged to the settled population as guardians of the Qur'an who followed the *shari'a*, even if some townspeople were little better than the nomads. The bedouin also saw Islam as the religion of the settled – whom they derided (Ibn Ghannam, 1949, 1:108, 163). Ibn 'Abd al-Wahhab claimed that even when one of the bedouin wanted to claim against another under the *shari'a*, the nomads still considered their customary law, which he labeled *hukm al-taghut* or "idol's judgment", i.e. without force or validity, to be the law of God (*haqq Allah*) (al-Rumi et al., eds, 1978, *Sira*, 39).

The element of tribal law that Ibn 'Abd al-Wahhab most disliked was tribal retaliation against a culprit's father, son, or other male relation (Ibn Ghannam, 1949, 1:108). This approach to legal accountability, grounded in communal responsibility and solidarity, presented a severe challenge to Wahhabi judges and Saudi *amir*s. It bred constant destabilizing feuding between rival bedouin elements, often carried down the generations. It stopped the Saudi authorities pinning legal accountability for killing or banditry on an individual tribesman without risk of conflict with his tribal section.

Nomads also ignored the provisions of the *shari'a* on marriage and divorce, property, and inheritance. Tribesmen took particular exception to those granting women rights of inheritance. They feared the detribalizing impact of property interests becoming misaligned with genealogical lines (ibid.; al-Rumi et al., eds, 1978, *RS*, 41). Ibn 'Abd al-Wahhab declared it illegitimate to pick and choose between Qur'anic prescriptions. If someone who generally observed Islamic prescriptions chose not to let women inherit contrary to the *shari'a*, he was guilty of unbelief. The determinant in any dispute had to be the word of God and His Prophet and of the people of learning, not popular custom (Ibn Ghannam, 1949, 1:113–14).

TAKFIR OF THE BEDOUIN

Ibn 'Abd al-Wahhab concluded that the bedouin had declared *takfir* of the Qur'an and the whole religion (al-Rumi et al., eds, 1978, *Sira*, 39). Their preference for customary law over the *shari'a* and failure, through worshiping idols and superstition, to observe *tawhid*, pray, and pay *zakat* made them infidels. They were guilty of a hundred infringements taking them beyond Islam, which they knew they were contravening (Ibn Ghannam, 1949, 1:108). They comprised a major part, if not the outright majority, of the local populace but that was beside the point. It did not make their practices any more religiously acceptable. Ibn 'Abd al-Wahhab resented their insults to the settled, singling out the 'Anaza and the al-Zafir, often allies of the Saudis' principal enemies, for special condemnation (ibid., 1:108, 144–5).

Ibn 'Abd al-Wahhab repudiated the view of clerics who conceded the bedouin were guilty of ignoring Islam but considered them saved from unbelief, and their lives and property exempted from *jihad*, by the *shahada*, the formal declaration that they were Muslims (ibid., 1:108, 163–4; al-Rumi et al., eds, 1978, *RS*, 41). He regarded this as a great untruth and its proponents as ignorant apostates. He preferred the words spoken to him by one nomad on hearing something of Islam: "I witness we are unbelievers (meaning he and all bedouin), and I witness that the teacher who calls us people of Islam is an unbeliever" (Rida, ed., 1999, 146).

Ibn 'Abd al-Wahhab issued an early *fatwa* pronouncing the unbelief of the bedouin and was at pains to justify this. He deployed a characteristic line of logic: if the Shi'a were unbelievers because of their excesses and despite their observance of much of Islam, how much more was this true of the bedouin whose only sign of Islam was recital of the *shahada* (al-Rumi et al., eds, 1978, *Sira*, 44)? This *fatwa*, which may have helped precipitate the struggle between Ibn 'Abd al-Wahhab and his critics, upset both populace and clerical opponents (Ibn Ghannam, 1949, 1:108–9; al-Rumi et al., eds, 1978, *RS*, 41–2). Ibn 'Abd al-Wahhab castigated the latter as enemies of God and wondered how they could declare the lives and property of Wahhabis forfeit yet the bedouin were inviolate just because they pronounced the *shahada* (al-Rumi et al., eds, 1978, *Sira*, 50). Most bedouin clearly rejected the *takfir* (Ibn Ghannam, 1949, 1:163–4).

TRIBALISM AND THE BEDOUIN

The Wahhabi campaign against tribal law as well as bedouin practices, such as quackery, can be portrayed as an attempt by the settled elite to assert their influence and authority over nomadic or pastoralist tribes. But there was no sharp distinction between settled and nomadic, between tribal and non-tribal. The depiction of society in the chronicles was colored by the same Wahhabi outlook that lay behind Ibn Ghannam's hyperbole in portraying the "era of ignorance". Ibn 'Abd al-Wahhab may even have used the label "bedouin" as invective against tribal targets who were settled.

Settlements around al-Dir'iyya were less tribalized than those elsewhere in Najd. Tribal structures had fragmented under the pressures of migration. Yet some towns remained prone to disintegration from rivalries between particular families, lineages, or tribal elements occupying separate quarters. Elsewhere townspeople might have long assumed tribal genealogies or tribal connections as a matter of political expediency and adopted aspects of tribal law. There was a complex caste system in settlements as among tribes.

Ibn 'Abd al-Wahhab had little sympathy for social hierarchies and scorned the snobbery associated with them (Ibn Ghannam, 1949, 1:202). He believed the only worthwhile distinction was between believers in *tawhid* and polytheists. The former constituted a brotherhood, irrespective of origin or social status. Yet he did not challenge such hierarchies directly and seems to have upheld the equality of the man's social status as a condition in marriage (*al-kafa'a fi-l-nasab*), as stipulated by all the law schools.

With tribal loyalties and customs prevalent in some settlements it was inevitable that some of the practices Ibn 'Abd al-Wahhab condemned were followed there, as among the bedouin. He observed that even some popular interpretations of the *shari'a* in settlements were based on custom, not solid textual foundation. Any cleric who had the temerity to contradict one of these interpretations, even in the most trivial matter, could find himself heavily criticized by the people. They would accuse him of innovation and refuse to perform prayer behind him (ibid., 1:114). Yet they remained curiously indifferent to major breaches of the *shari'a*.

Inevitably, Ibn 'Abd al-Wahhab's *takfir* of the bedouin aroused opposition even among settled elements. Some might have welcomed support against bedouin pressure. But in the short term to anathematize the bedouin risked the viability and, in some cases, cohesion of settlements. Traders had cause to fear for their lines of supply, just as Hijazi notables and clerics engaged in the pilgrimage business worried about the integrity of pilgrim routes that were always susceptible to brigandage and extortion by nomads. Two of the Al Sa'ud's greatest rivals, the Bani Khalid in the eighteenth century and the Al Rashid of Hail in the later nineteenth and early twentieth centuries, headed tribal confederations comprised of both settled population and nomads. The Bani Khalid also had Shi'i tribal sections, as did some other tribes in western Arabia, such as the Harb.

Ibn 'Abd al-Wahhab did not address directly in his writings the legitimacy of the tribute paid to bedouin by the settled population, whether exacted under a traditional arrangement or extorted by duress as protection money. However, requiring common submission to them as enforcers of God's law, Saudi rulers would have expected direct payment of tribute to them in the form of *zakat*. They would have disallowed hierarchical arrangements involving tribute between settlements or between the settlements and nomadic tribes. As part of a sustained campaign to secure lines of communication, they worked to abolish levies on travelers traditionally imposed by bedouin who demanded they took a tribal escort. The Saudis realized that buying off the bedouin had limited effect. So they applied force to discipline the tribes, with considerable success. They regarded safety on the roads as one of their major objectives and achievements (Ibn Bishr, 1982–3, 1:268–72).

Ironically the Saudis coopted the bedouin finally in the last years of the eighteenth century. They replaced tribal collection of protection money with a Saudi toll. They recompensed the tribes for their loss of income from tribal raiding with booty from officially sponsored campaigns. Hardy bedouin elements played an important role in Saudi military successes as the Wahhabis moved into the Hijaz, Yemen, and Iraq, as well as in the massacre that occurred when the Saudis overran the Shi'i holy city of Karbala in 1802. They sacked the Sunni town of Taif with unbridled savagery and vandalism in early 1803. As Wahhabi outriders, they participated in Saudi raids that appeared to threaten even Cairo, Damascus, and Baghdad. Some of their actions damaged the reputation of Wahhabism, confirming the stereotypical image that those cities' inhabitants had of the Wahhabis as uncivilized desert nomads.

When the Egyptian invasion finally came, the opportunistic bedouin proved unreliable allies for Wahhabi townspeople. They fell easy prey to the bribery and pressure wielded by the invaders, and succumbed readily to the temptation to re-embrace their old predatory way of life. They turned out to be just the kind of hypocrites Ibn 'Abd al-Wahhab had warned against. They remained thorns in the flesh of all Saudi rulers until settled in encampments after 1912. The most recalcitrant of their leaders were finally subjugated militarily by Ibn Sa'ud in 1929.

HOLY MEN, CULTS, AND SUFIS

Ibn 'Abd al-Wahhab insisted on God's absolute power independent of the universe (transcendence). He was deeply opposed to the immanentist tradition, which had God present in the physical world and so accessible through intercession, local cults, and Sufi practices. He viewed this outlook as marked by superstition and obscurantism. Such corruptions of Islam contravened *tawhid* and were impermissible in any form: "whoever creates intermediaries between himself and God to whom he prays, asks for intercession and places his trust has committed unbelief by consensus" (Rida, ed., 1999, 177). Associating another person or thing with God took the individual beyond Islam, even when his motives were pious and he wanted only to get closer to God (al-Rumi et al., eds, 1978, *'Aqida*, 1:399). Humans, alive or dead, were not to be credited with any facet of divinity (Ibn Ghannam, 1949, 1:116–17). Although the Prophet was exceptionally a valid intercessor (al-Rumi et al., eds, 1978, *RS*, 48–9), even he had no share of divinity (ibid., 9–10).

Ibn 'Abd al-Wahhab acknowledged the miracles and revelations of saints. He ruled out according them any power. This belonged exclusively to God. Belief in, and veneration of, saints was equivalent to the worship of idols (Ibn Ghannam, 1949, 1:215–18). Praying to a Muslim saint was to make a god of him. All the festivals and rituals at saints' tombs amounted to worship of idols warranting *takfir* (ibid., 1:164). He condemned the Sufi practice of remembrance (*dhikr*), a spiritual exercise designed to infuse oneself with God's presence, as an innovation that was by definition illegitimate (ibid., 1:143), as well as two prayer books beloved of Sufis (though he denied having either burnt) (al-Rumi et al., eds, 1978, *RS*, 12). He disliked and distrusted Sufis' concern with the individual's spiritual salvation at the expense of the proper regulation of the community, and their focus on the next world instead of on implementing God's law and will in this. The result was that many spiritual Muslims found Wahhabi dogma emotionally stark, cheerless, and unforgiving.

Ibn 'Abd al-Wahhab's confrontation with his opponents was sparked by a *fatwa* he issued early in his campaign. Distributed and publicized against his wishes, this condemned local holy men,

...e feared holy man from al-Kharj who used to visit ...nen were the worst idolaters and made the poly-...orse than the unbelievers in the Prophet's time, a ...his writings (e.g. ibid., 125). They infringed both ...were apostates. Anyone who worshiped them was patently an unbeliever (Crawford, 2011, 150–1). If this *takfir* of these holy men was controversial, he compounded the impact by declining, in castigating practices associated with tombs or shrines, to distinguish between local holy men, Sufi saints, pious ancestors, Companions of the Prophet, and the Prophet himself. Worship of kings, prophets, saints, trees, stones, wood, graves, or jinns all amounted to the same thing – polytheism with the penalty of eternal hellfire (al-Rumi et al., eds, 1978, *RS*, 146, 154; Rida, ed., 1928, 4:18–19).

This *fatwa* placed Sunnis of the moderate and sober Qadiriyya Sufi order at the same level of unbelief as the Rafidites (i.e. the Shi'a) (Ibn Ghannam, 1949, 1:167) and Christians, although only the latter were innocent of apostasy. This was striking because all the three major Hanbalis who had most influenced him, namely Ibn Taymiyya, Ibn al-Qayyim, and the jurist Ibn Qudama, may have been Qadiris. Ibn 'Abd al-Wahhab denied, unconvincingly, that he had excommunicated the famous Muslim mystics Ibn al-'Arabi (d. 1240) and Ibn al-Farid (d. 1235) (al-Rumi et al., eds, 1978, *RS*, 12), but he loathed their creeds as worse unbelief than that of the Jews and Christians (Ibn Ghannam, 1949, 1:147–8). He resisted attempts to rehabilitate them or reconcile their views with the *shari'a*. It doubtless disturbed him to discover his maternal grandfather's linkage to Ibn al-'Arabi.

Always hostile to spiritual hierarchies, the early Wahhabis were scathing about the pretensions of holy men who sought to make a special caste of themselves. Ruler 'Abd al-'Aziz wrote:

> The saint (*wali*) in this age has become someone who has lengthened his rosary and widened his sleeves, lets his shawl hang down, extends his hand to be kissed, dresses in distinctive clothes, assembles drums and banners, and consumes the funds of God's creatures in oppression and pretension, despite the *Sunna* of the Chosen One [the Prophet] and the provisions of his law.
>
> (Ibn Sihman, ed., 1925/6, 12)

Ibn 'Abd al-Wahhab saw popular infatuation with the superstitious falsities of these frauds as enabling them to prey on common people. The latter squandered precious money on donations and offerings, the purchase of amulets or talismans, visitation and decoration of saints' tombs, and folk rituals. This was money they should have dedicated to mosque-building and *jihad* (Rida, ed., 1999, 351). Even local clerics participated in Sufi and folk festivals and tried to benefit by claiming to perform miracles themselves (Ibn Qasim, ed., 1996–9, 1:54). The early Wahhabis' animus against saints' trappings and accessories helps explain their strict ban on luxury, music, tobacco, and narcotics. Stamina-inducing stimulants were an established feature of Sufi gatherings.

Actual Sufis have an oddly shadowy presence in Ibn 'Abd al-Wahhab's Najd. His letters and writings rarely mention specific contemporary Sufis, Sufi orders, or indeed Sufism in a Najdi context. He did encounter Sufis in the Holy Cities and probably also in Basra and al-Ahsa. There are no direct hints of active and established Sufi orders in Najd beyond references to a few Ibn al-'Arabi followers in hostile Riyadh, the possible influence of the small family-based 'Aydarus order derived from the Hadramawt in Yemen and, obliquely, the popularity of the Qadiriyya order in Najd. Sufis were more real among Ibn 'Abd al-Wahhab's regional enemies. Ahmad al-Qabbani based at the Shadhili al-Kawwaz mosque in Basra wrote as many as three early anti-Wahhabi refutations that Ibn 'Abd al-Wahhab much resented (Ibn Ghannam, 1949, 1:106).

Wahhabi writings fail to mention the destruction of specifically Sufi shrines in Najd or Wahhabi hounding of specifically Sufi adherents in the early decades. This suggests if the mystic orders existed at all in Najd, it was only in a highly degraded form that Ibn 'Abd al-Wahhab could or would not distinguish from folk religiosity. His mild father issued a condemnation of dervish practices in Najd that included walking through fire, jumping from roofs, and beating themselves with iron, practices he considered derived from the Zoroastrians. He noted that the dervishes ascribed these practices to 'Abd al-Qadir al-Jilani, "one of the greatest of clerics among God's saints", who had in fact opposed such excesses (Rida, ed., 1928, 1:523–5).

Hanbalis had traditionally condemned certain Sufi practices. Ibn 'Abd al-Wahhab went further with an unqualified attack on the veneration of shrines or living human beings. Later the Wahhabi position on Sufism mellowed, suggesting no absolute incompatibility of Wahhabism and Sufism. Some Sufis not only survived Saudi rule in the Hijaz in the early nineteenth century but established personal links to the Al Sa'ud. On the conquest of Mecca Shaykh 'Abd Allah, son of Ibn 'Abd al-Wahhab, even declared acceptable Sufi orders that observed orthodoxy and orthopraxy (as interpreted by the Wahhabis) (Mouline, 2011, 101).

Mutual antagonism between Sufis and Wahhabis contributed significantly to the regional Wahhabi controversy that erupted from 1742 onward. It became acute in the case of the Naqshbandiyya. On the face of it this order and Wahhabism shared common features. Both insisted on the performance of religious duties. Both had a strongly Sunni complexion and a tendency, especially in the case of the renewed Naqshbandiyya of the nineteenth century, to political activism. However, the Naqshbandis were closely associated with the Ottomans and resented what they saw as Saudi rebellion against Ottoman authority. It was a reformist Naqshbandi *mufti* of Islam in Istanbul who oversaw the execution of the Saudi Imam 'Abd Allah there in December 1818 after Egyptian forces had conquered al-Dir'iyya. Turkey, where the Naqshbandiyya remains strong, became a center for anti-Wahhabi propaganda.

THE SHI'A

For Ibn 'Abd al-Wahhab the fourth source of corruption threatening the true religion was Shi'ism. This was arguably as insidious as malevolent or misguided clerics, tribal practices, holy men, or popular mystics. It was potentially more dangerous. Hostility to Shi'a was natural for Hanbalis. Their doctrinal approach rested heavily on Prophetic traditions transmitted by Companions. The Shi'a believed many of these took the wrong side of the dispute with the Caliph 'Ali and discounted them as unreliable or worse. In early Wahhabi demonology the Shi'a were archetypical associationists and deserved particular condemnation for attributing special powers or aspects of divinity to 'Ali and his offspring. They were among the enemies of God and the Prophet (al-Rumi et al., eds, 1978, *RS*, 97). Anyone who doubted their unbelief was himself an unbeliever (Ibn Ghannam, 1949, 1:141).

Ibn 'Abd al-Wahhab regarded the Rafidites as the worst of the Shi'a. For they had introduced polytheism into the Muslim community, disowned the caliphs other than 'Ali, regarded many of the Prophet's Companions as apostates, and insulted them (ibid., 1:152). He did not distinguish between categories or varieties of Shi'a, as Ibn Taymiyya had. He included all Shi'a under the Rafidite rubric. They were all guilty of dissimulation (*taqiyya*), illegitimate practices such as temporary marriage, and hostility to Sunnis. Their excesses and subversion of the Qur'an made them worse than the Jews or Christians, whom to an extent they resembled.

There were no Shi'a in Najd but they constituted three-quarters of the population of the upper Gulf region, including eastern Arabia around al-Ahsa and in Bahrain. They were also to be found among both settled population and tribes in the west, and in Medina itself. The Wahhabis (and some other Sunnis) suspected the Hashimite Sharifs of Mecca of being crypto-Shi'a who could not be trusted to uphold Sunnism. We have seen that fear of Shi'ism may have helped spark Ibn 'Abd al-Wahhab's original campaign in Basra against the background of Nader Shah's insidious attempt to resolve the great schism in Islam. He later indicated to an Iraqi correspondent that he would never accept rapprochement with polytheists, least of all with the "cursed Rafidites" (ibid., 1:152).

This deep hostility to the Shi'a manifested itself in the later years of the First Saudi State in the sacking of Karbala by the Wahhabis in 1802 when thousands died. The Saudis also tried the year after Ibn 'Abd al-Wahhab's death to destroy all signs of Shi'ism in the al-Ahsa region and to instruct Shi'i inhabitants in *tawhid*, the four Sunni schools, and the foundations of Islam (Ibn Ghannam, 1949, 2:159–61; Ibn Bishr, 1982–3, 1:202–3). This was the start of an intermittent Saudi campaign to convert local Shi'a to a Wahhabi version of Sunnism that proved singularly unsuccessful. Over time, to the frustration of some clerics, Saudi rulers became more pragmatic and merely suppressed public manifestations of Shi'ism while discriminating against Shi'a politically and economically.

At an ideological level, in raising the banner of *tawhid*, "Wahhābism represented the greatest fundamentalist challenge to Shī'īsm since the beginning of Islam" (Enayat, 1982, 41). It stimulated a powerful strain of anti-Shi'ism among Salafis in the late twentieth and early twenty-first centuries and generated an antagonism between the Saudis and the state in Shi'i Iran that became an enduring reality for Gulf inhabitants.

7

THE REGIME OF GODLINESS AND THE POLITICAL ORDER

The outline in chapter 2 of Ibn 'Abd al-Wahhab's earlier career described how he launched his movement of religious purification some years before merging its fate with that of the Al Sa'ud. Although the Saudis had been rulers of the settlement of al-Dir'iyya for decades, the arrangement he made in 1744/5 with Muhammad ibn Sa'ud marks for modern historians the start of the First Saudi State. This did not in itself make the settlement any more a "state" in the modern sense than it was before.

The arrangement between *shaykh* and ruler may have set over time rather than been sealed in the one dramatic encounter of legend. Likewise it took many years for the polity based on al-Dir'iyya to evolve into something resembling a Saudi state. Some of the First Saudi State's most distinctive features, including the imamate and the division of responsibilities between Al Sa'ud and clerics, took shape only in its last phase, though chroniclers and modern historians often projected them back in time.

EXPLAINING THE GENESIS OF WAHHABISM

Questions hover over the origins of Wahhabism: why then? why there? and why in that form? One attractive thesis argues that early Wahhabism was a response to Najd's need for improved governance and represented a state-forming project (al-Fahad, 2004a, 487). A variation suggests it was as much about politics as religion and supplied an ideology of state formation.

This chapter considers the role of Wahhabism and the nature of governance in the Saudi state by looking at four propositions associated with this broad thesis: first, that social and economic developments across Najd in the early eighteenth century created a demand for an end to political fragmentation and for a unitary government to manage scarce resources more effectively; second, that, as the product of "a stateless society", the Wahhabi movement had "the explicit purpose of forming a state" (ibid.); third, that this impulse to build a new state drew on Ibn 'Abd al-Wahhab's thinking on the political order so that this shaped the conceptual and institutional foundations of the First Saudi State; and finally, and more nebulously, that other doctrinal aspects of Wahhabism contributed to the process of state formation.

We should remain cautious here about the term "state". Today's notion of the state would have been unfamiliar to Ibn 'Abd al-Wahhab. In his time the Arabic word for "state" (*dawla*) applied to few regional powers, preeminent among them the Ottoman empire. It was only in the final phase of the First Saudi State that the term *dawla* can be found in Wahhabi writings referring to the growing Saudi empire ruled out of al-Dir'iyya (Rida, ed., 1928, 4:574). Even then it embodied ideas of sovereignty and borders markedly different from those we associate today with the term "state".

SOCIAL AND ECONOMIC TRENDS

Put cogently in an original work by Juhany, the case for social, economic, and educational developments in Najd stimulating a unifying movement in the form of Wahhabism rests on the argument that migration movements and settlement, the growth of the sedentary population, and the increase in the number and spread of clerics in the three centuries before Wahhabism created a new situation in Najd. Fierce competition for scarce resources caused persistent conflict and political fragmentation. These created a powerful pent-up demand for a central government to impose order and justice, manage resources, and create a unified community (Juhany, 2002, 160–3).

The secularly trained mind of today is more comfortable with this idea of Wahhabism as the product and reflection of social and economic trends than of religious inspiration and one individual's determination. We are uneasy with an explanation that ascribes Wahhabism to "an act of God", or with the concept of a "great man" changing the course of regional history, albeit as God's instrument. Hostile contemporaries too struggled with the notion of Ibn 'Abd al-Wahhab as solely responsible for Wahhabism. Hence the later charge that he was the agent of external political forces.

The difficulty with Juhany's attractive thesis lies in the incompleteness and ambiguity of some of the evidence. In particular, there are inadequate data for periods before the late seventeenth century to enable comparisons. Large, uneven movements of settled and nomadic populations from the Yemen region across the Peninsula to its northern and eastern peripheries had long been a feature of regional demographics. These waves, which worked their way through over generations, always placed pressure on resources. Wahhabism may have been stimulated by growth in the sedentary population in Najd and the need for better ordering of government and society. We just cannot be sure from the evidence we have.

Less persuasive is the more dramatic view that "Najd of the eighteenth century was a disintegrating society. It was on the verge of collapse" (al-Dakhil, 2009, 28). The supporting evidence includes cycles of internal strife in settlements, wars between them, assassinations, droughts, and so on. But fragmentary annals suggest that this too was the pattern for previous centuries, though we have less detail for them than for the seventeenth and eighteenth centuries. Many of these recurrent phenomena have a timeless quality. It is telling how fast previous political and social habits reasserted themselves after the fall of al-Dir'iyya in 1818, almost as if the Saudi state had never been. The narrower claim that a long-term trend of detribalization was intensifying levels of local instability and creating demand for a new form of social glue in an increasingly fissiparous society is more convincing (see al-Fahad, 2004b, 37).

STATE FORMATION AND THE REGIME OF GODLINESS

The advocate of the view that Najd was heading for unprecedented political disintegration describes "nation building" as "a declared objective of the shaikh all along" (al-Dakhil, 2009, 28). This raises the question squarely whether Ibn 'Abd al-Wahhab's initial aim was indeed to create a state, which would be a prerequisite for developing a "nation".

Ibn 'Abd al-Wahhab's pre-Saudi career included campaigns on Ottoman territory and then in a Najdi town without overall political leadership. This does not point to such an ambition. In al-'Uyayna his goal was limited to establishing a local regime of godliness where God's law would be respected and enforced. He did not seek to usurp political power nor to start an insurgency against other rulers with the objective of overturning the political status quo by force (Crawford, 2011, 160).

Ibn 'Abd al-Wahhab's ambitions once in al-Dir'iyya expanded with political and military success. His original outlook had been cramped and focused on al-'Arid, his home area of Najd. His initial aim was not to establish a state in a conventional sense, let alone a nation. It was to institute a regime of godliness. He appreciated that this depended on enforcement by the local ruler. It would take more than fine preaching to convince people to change their religious practices and pray in congregation five times a day.

It was the collective effort to install and defend this regime in al-Dir'iyya that caused the emergence of a new kind of state. This was largely the outcome of the interplay between local forces in Najd in the decades after 1744 and the need for the Saudis to wage uninterrupted warfare over decades. The First Saudi State certainly never embodied any kind of "nationhood". This was an entirely foreign concept to Ibn 'Abd al-Wahhab with his universal religious message, as well as to his Najdi contemporaries.

Absolutist in theology, Ibn 'Abd al-Wahhab was a realist in politics and declined to make the best the enemy of the good. Like many Salafis since, he considered a regime of godliness could be introduced on a small scale, regardless of wider political frameworks or governance issues. He could have held that he was unable to implement his vision of Islamic society in the absence of an overarching Islamic political authority. This was the stance of clerics who condemned his stoning of the adulterous woman in al-'Uyayna. They claimed he lacked the authority to inflict one of the severest punishments (*hudud*) of Islamic law. This was illegitimate in the absence of a supreme *imam* or ruler of the Muslims (Ibn Ghannam, 1949, 1:207).

Ibn 'Abd al-Wahhab retorted that there had not been such a supreme *imam* since before even Ibn Hanbal. One had to be realistic about the exercise of political power and authority or else the world would be left unregulated, without rules, political order, or exercise of judicial authority (ibid., 1:203, 207). Like Ibn Taymiyya (and the Kharijites), he saw no canonical requirement for a supreme *imam* or caliph. Valid power rested with any ruler, irrespective of social background (an Abyssinian slave would do), who applied the *shari'a* and ordered the right and forbade the wrong. There could be no true religion without such a ruler, whose task was to lead the community (*jama'a*) even if his domains amounted to just a town or two (ibid., 1:207).

Once in al-'Uyayna or al-Dir'iyya, Ibn 'Abd al-Wahhab appreciated his good fortune in not having to adapt to the realities of an already established and powerful state, unlike regional reformers who had to suffer the Ottomans. Exploiting his relationship with the local ruler, he could implement his regime, irrespective of practice elsewhere or the hostility of other local rulers or inhabitants (Rida, ed., 1928, 4:2).

A local ruler was necessary not just to enforce the *shari'a* and precepts of *tawhid*, but to ensure communal and individual observance of wider Islamic norms. This involved "commanding right and forbidding wrong", a well-established Islamic concept that Ibn 'Abd al-Wahhab endorsed and which today is reflected in the activities of the Saudi "religious police" (*mutawwi'in*).

By Ibn 'Abd al-Wahhab's definition, the most important and obligatory aspect of "right", the first duty imposed by God, was "*tawhid* and *tawhid*" (Ibn Qasim, ed., 1996–9, 1:168). *Tawhid* separated true believers from polytheists whereas, conventionally, the more mundane concept of commanding right was aimed at those who did not perform their religious duties or sinned in ways that did not necessarily take them beyond the community. Ibn 'Abd al-Wahhab cared about practical enforcement of norms but was ideologically more interested in major doctrinal infractions than everyday sinning. This explains why he employed the traditional language of commanding right and forbidding wrong relatively infrequently in his formal writings. The dynamic concept of *tawhid* in action exerted more ideological and polemical force.

Anti-Wahhabis latched onto this doctrinal emphasis. Early on they deployed the slur that Ibn 'Abd al-Wahhab did not concern himself with non-Muslim unbelievers; nor did he care about those who committed adultery or drank alcohol. Instead he reserved his opprobrium for those who believed in saints (Traboulsi, 2002, 402). In his critics' eyes, he was divisive and indifferent to external threats to the Islamic world. He also disregarded the nefarious activities of those he classed as genuine Wahhabis. So long as they were his followers and doctrinally compliant, he was indifferent to their ill-conduct (Ibn Ghannam, 1949, 1:112). This accusation gained greater force once illiterate, rapacious bedouin started raiding beyond Najd for the Saudis in Ibn 'Abd al-Wahhab's final years.

COMMANDING RIGHT AND FORBIDDING WRONG

In reality, *tawhid* in action did not displace or exclude routine commanding of right in Saudi-governed settlements. The daily enforcement of Wahhabi norms, including prayers in congregation, and the censorious, fearful atmosphere it instilled were something non-Wahhabis under Saudi occupation found oppressive and resented. Wavering rulers, confronted by Saudi pressure, feared the divisive impact such a regime would have in their own communities, even if these did not include Shi'a. Ibn 'Abd al-Wahhab recognized the potential for trouble. He laid down various requirements for enforcement: whoever commanded right should be knowledgeable in religion, mild in applying the rules, and ready for potential blowback from enforcement (ibid., 1:171).

Initially Ibn 'Abd al-Wahhab and senior *shaykh*s were involved in commanding right. Once the Saudi polity was better organized, the monitoring, encouraging, and policing of communal and individual observance of Islamic norms, including prayer five times a day, became a matter for the Al Sa'ud, assisted by local *amir*s (equivalent to governors), *imam*s of mosques, and volunteer enforcers (*mutawwi'in*).

Communal enforcement was preeminently about regulation of the public sphere. However, the early Wahhabis were less wedded to the distinction between public and private than earlier Hanbalis and less concerned to restrain the interfering busybody. The communal system required the individual Wahhabi to subordinate his interests to the wider communal good. It needed Wahhabi precepts to regulate his relationship with non-Muslims or polytheists. A rare reference to the Muslim's private space offers a revealing insight into Ibn 'Abd al-Wahhab's own priorities. He declared it more important for the Muslim to teach his family and household to display enmity, not friendship, to disbelievers than to instruct them in ritual purity and prayer (al-Rumi et al., eds, 1978, *RS*, 322–3).

Advocate as he was of interventionism in the public space, Ibn 'Abd al-Wahhab at no point discusses in his writings how best to organize communal enforcement in practice. The chronicles make no mention of bodies for commanding right organized, appointed, or supported by the government in Najd during the First Saudi State. Instead it was the duty of every right-believing member of society, irrespective of rank, to command right and forbid wrong (Ibn Qasim, ed., 1996–9, 14:20–1, 27, 38, 45–6). There were no exemptions or excuses. All believers shared responsibility for the proper regulation of society. They were not to be deterred by fear or consideration for someone (ibid., 14:53). The Saudis not only urged Wahhabis to inform on each other, but insisted they had a duty to inform once the culprit had disregarded a warning. Otherwise they would be complicit (Rida, ed., 1928, 1:19).

Relying on the most pious in the community to enforce Wahhabi norms carried risks. Ibn 'Abd al-Wahhab claimed personal experience of an excess of zeal among self-appointed guardians of morality undermining the unity of the local community. For him communal solidarity took priority over rigorous enforcement. Wary of repeating the mistakes of the Kharijites, he told followers that for one group of Wahhabis to condemn another for laxity in enforcing the rules, or for Wahhabis to criticize the local *amir* for the way he commanded right, risked splitting the community. Wahhabis should not push enthusiasm for forbidding wrong to this point. This would cause disputes among themselves or damage the political interests of Wahhabism (Ibn Ghannam, 1949, 1:171). Episodes in the twentieth century demonstrated Ibn 'Abd al-Wahhab's prescience.

It was probably to diminish the likelihood of such an outcome that the early Al Sa'ud gave primary, but not exclusive, responsibility for enforcement to local *amir*s acting in concert with "the people of religion" (Ibn Qasim, ed., 1996–9, 14:23). There remained a risk in the Wahhabi's duty to command right and forbid wrong. It gave him locus in local governance and potential license to contest Saudi decisions. In tackling potential strains between local Saudi authorities and zealots, ruler and *shaykh* relied on a network of reliable judges to help keep settlements clear of dissension.

Ibn 'Abd al-Wahhab's guidance was that if the *amir* of a town or someone in authority did something wrong, he should be cautioned, gently and in private. If he accepted and acted on the advice, there was no need to advertise the matter. If not, the condemnation and background to it could be publicized. If the *amir* still did not concede, the matter should be elevated to Ibn 'Abd al-Wahhab secretly (Ibn Ghannam, 1949, 1:171). The chronicles record numerous examples of ruler 'Abd al-'Aziz and Ibn 'Abd al-Wahhab responding to local concerns about the conduct of *amir*s by rushing to dismiss them and replace them with others, generally from among local notables, before anti-Wahhabis could profit.

GOVERNMENT AND THE POLITICAL ORDER

If Ibn 'Abd al-Wahhab had aimed explicitly to form a state rather than establish a local regime of godliness, we might have expected conceptual thinking from him on the proper organization of Islamic government and society, especially in a specifically Najdi and Saudi context. Curiously for someone so prescriptive in doctrinal matters, he devoted no attention to this. Nor did he express his ideas in explicitly political language. In all his letters and writings there is barely a mention of the Al Sa'ud or its wider Al Muqrin clan.

Ibn 'Abd al-Wahhab's thinking on government was unoriginal and unsophisticated. Political power was in the service of religion, not the other way round. The ruler's task was to uphold *tawhid* and the *shari'a* and to reject innovations. Any ruler who changed God's law or did not govern in line with the Qur'an and *Sunna* became an idol (*taghut*) (Rida, ed., 1999, 161). Partly because of its association with oppression (*tughyan*), this term had the potential to import a dynamic concept into Wahhabi thought. Ibn 'Abd al-Wahhab did not alight on it but fell back on quietist Sunni doctrine. The community of Muslims had to give unreserved obedience to the ruler if supported by the notables, however tyrannical he was, even if of no or low social standing, provided he did not order disobedience to God (al-Rumi et al., eds, 1978, *RS*, 11).

Ibn 'Abd al-Wahhab placed an entirely conventional premium on communal solidarity in the political sphere, even at the price of tyrannical government. This was odd for a cleric who could visualize truth as lying with one individual and not the majority and who found the prevailing religious consensus oppressive. He associated dissension and subversion with polytheism, and political fragmentation with religious divisions and distinctions based on special hierarchies and groupings. On his reading of the era of ignorance, opposition to the ruler was a virtue and obedience signified degradation and humiliation (Rida, ed., 1999, 126).

Under the regime of godliness *tawhid* and communal unity were interlocking. Socially and politically, *tawhid* was the citadel around which the people rallied, and the community was held together by the presence of a ruler entitled to total obedience. This stress on unity and obedience reflected in part Ibn 'Abd al-Wahhab's concern with doctrinal discipline. This was a matter for the whole Wahhabi community. The religious *shaykhs* policed the theological boundaries. Saudi rulers, *amirs*, and Wahhabi volunteers enforced the regime of godliness on the individual to help guarantee his salvation, whether he liked it or not.

A symbolic but significant reflection of the Wahhabi approach to unity was the requirement not just that prayers be communal rather than performed on one's own or at home, but that communal prayers be held correctly (al-Jabarti, 1958–67, 6:76). This meant in one body. This caused consternation and confusion among Hijazi clerics when the Saudis occupied Mecca in 1803. They expected Hanbali bigotry. Instead they were faced by the Wahhabi ruler's order that all the Sunni schools pray at the same time in the Great Mosque, led by *imams* from any of the four schools, instead of praying separately at different times under their own *imams*, as was the previous practice (Dahlan, 1887/8, 278–9). Critics took this as further evidence of the Wahhabis working to ignore or dissolve the schools.

OBEDIENCE TO THE RULER

Ibn 'Abd al-Wahhab complained that contemporary clerics did not understand or act on the principle of obedience. To obey clerics and *amirs* in forbidding what God allowed and allowing what God forbade made them lords to the exclusion of God (Rida, ed., 1999, 68). Yet he never resolved the awkward issue for the conventional doctrine of authoritarian government of the ruler failing to perform as religious precepts demanded. Nor did he address satisfactorily the question at what point Muslims were relieved of their duty to obey and when rebellion was justified. In theory this was when the ruler became an openly declared unbeliever or ordered disobedience to God, but when did he become a tyrant acting in disregard of God's law (i.e. a *taghut*)? What about a ruler who was merely lax in his personal conduct or in enforcing Islamic norms?

When it came to Saudi insurgency campaigns launched from al-Dir'iyya after 1746, a different approach applied to anti-Wahhabis. A formal Wahhabi verdict of apostasy on a ruler absolved his subjects of any duty to obey. Ibn 'Abd al-Wahhab treated the assassination of 'Uthman ibn Mu'ammar by pro-Wahhabi notables in al-'Uyayna as a legitimate, if awkward, deed. Likewise, if a whole settlement or its ruler was subject to *takfir*, local Wahhabis had not only a right but the duty to overthrow the existing political order and kill the ruler.

Where Najdi settlements submitted to al-Dir'iyya or the Saudis occupied them after a fight, the Saudi ruler either confirmed the local ruler or appointed a new one who could then expect full obedience. Once the Saudis moved beyond Najd and lacked the military resources and support from local Wahhabis to ensure domination, they then showed more concern with the proper regulation of religion and society than with exercising sovereignty or imposing their own rule in place of the pre-existing system of government. They were inclined to confirm local rulers and judges in office, despite doubting their political and religious loyalties, provided they undertook to enforce the regime of godliness with Wahhabi support. If they did that, those rulers could expect obedience, albeit wary and provisional.

In the case of the Al Sa'ud a rule of absolute obedience applied. Hamad ibn Nasir (d. 1811), the leading Wahhabi jurist of the First Saudi State, was not only a pupil of Ibn 'Abd al-Wahhab but ironically 'Uthman ibn Mu'ammar's grandson. In a passage redolent of Christian thinking, he advised the individual Muslim to render unto *amir*s what was their due and ask God for what was due the Muslim. There was great virtue, he declared, in bearing what was reprehensible (Ibn Qasim, ed., 1996–9, 9:236–7). How reprehensible conduct of government would have to be to nullify the duty of obedience was not tested with the Al Sa'ud until the later nineteenth century.

The Wahhabis were fortunate in their early rulers. Muhammad ibn Sa'ud may have been conventionally minded and of limited vision but he was stalwart and respected (Ibn Ghannam, 1949, 2:3). The next three generations of rulers until the state's demise in 1818 were dedicated Wahhabis whose personal behavior and conduct of government never aroused concerns about disobedience to God or tyranny. The only dissent among the Al Sa'ud that manifested itself in this period was possibly during the final reign of 'Abd Allah when uncles may have contested his succession but the evidence for this is slight.

What could clerics do if rulers left the straight and narrow? Ibn 'Abd al-Wahhab offered the sole expedient of cautionary and non-binding advice. This unformalized means of influence rested crucially on the status of the cleric offering it and the readiness of the ruler to listen. Ibn 'Abd al-Wahhab's published correspondence contains no examples of specific advice to rulers, whether Al Sa'ud or hostile. Presumably he delivered advice to Saudi leaders privately in al-Dir'iyya to ensure no loss of face. The Saudis handled political opponents, waverers, or miscreants directly, leaving Ibn 'Abd al-Wahhab to attend to the clerical ranks.

Ibn 'Abd al-Wahhab thus offered no overt behavioral models for intervention by clerics or others should a ruler ignore or contravene the *shari'a*. The notion of commanding right and forbidding wrong offered a potential conceptual basis for intervention in the public space. Yet he made clear, when this threatened dissension, that it was subject to the religion's and community's wider interest in unity. As a result he supplied no means for the Saudi state to accommodate political criticism, other than that delivered through private advice, without it acquiring the dangerous label of illegitimate rebellion. The unsophisticated nature of the Wahhabi polity with its premium on unity and lack of political safety valves made it vulnerable to fracture once exposed to the military and economic stresses of the Egyptian invasion.

PRINCES AND CLERICS

In the end there was a clear delineation of responsibilities between the Al Sa'ud and the Wahhabi religious establishment. The Al Sa'ud exercised all political, military, and executive decision-making functions, as well as commanded right, upheld and enforced justice, and issued guidance, based on Wahhabi values, to the people. The clerics, headed by Ibn 'Abd al-Wahhab and his descendants, the Al al-Shaykh, offered religious guidance to the ruler, *amir*s, and people in public through teaching, sermons, and gatherings in the *majlis*. They administered justice and gave the ruler non-binding advice on conduct of government.

This balanced partnership echoes an arrangement envisaged by Ibn Taymiyya in his work *Public administration under the shari'a (al-Siyasa al-shar'iyya*). It is curious that Ibn 'Abd al-Wahhab, who quoted liberally from Ibn Taymiyya's writings, does not appear to refer to this work. The early Wahhabis never conceptualized the demarcation of spheres of authority between clerics and princes. It took decades to develop and seems to have taken shape only once Ibn 'Abd al-Wahhab withdrew from day-to-day involvement in state business in 1773/4.

Immediately after 1744 Ibn 'Abd al-Wahhab, as founder of the embattled Wahhabi movement, was intimately concerned with government. In Huraymila he had himself received the formal allegiance (*bay'a*) of his vanguard of believers (Ibn Ghannam, 1949, 1:29). This occurred in al-'Uyayna also (Ibn Bishr, 1982–3, 1:43). On arrival in al-Dir'iyya he and Muhammad ibn Sa'ud exchanged vows of allegiance and commitment to God's law. Thereafter, those submitting appear to have given their oath to the *shaykh* alone (e.g. ibid., 1:48). Later a pattern developed of individuals and settlements giving their covenant of allegiance, including undertaking to wage *jihad*, to both ruler and *shaykh* right up until the latter's death. Contrary to Hanbali doctrine that he himself espoused, Ibn 'Abd al-Wahhab, not Muhammad ibn Sa'ud, declared offensive *jihad* in about 1746 (ibid., 1:45–6, 48).

During the first decades after 1744 the *shaykh* was involved in all important policy decisions, especially at times of crisis, and in appointing *amir*s (as in al-'Uyayna after 'Uthman's assassination). He also ran the treasury throughout this period. He played a key role in dividing plunder from Saudi military campaigning and deciding on religious and welfare spending of funds collected as alms (*zakat*) (ibid., 1:46). Ibn 'Abd al-Wahhab surrendered this role to 'Abd al-'Aziz when he scaled back government engagement to teach and write (ibid., 1:46–7).

The clear separation of roles between the Al Sa'ud and the clerics began to take shape in the interval between the *shaykh*'s retirement from front-line politics in 1773/4 and his death in 1792. The divide in function was already symbolized geographically. The Al Sa'ud lived on the west side of the Wadi Hanifa in the al-Turayf quarter of al-Dir'iyya. Ibn 'Abd al-Wahhab and his family (the Al al-Shaykh) remained across the wadi in the al-Bujayri district. No members of the Al Sa'ud in this era, however pious, became *mufti*s or *qadi*s. None of the Al al-Shaykh went into politics or became *amirs*. Some Al Saʿud attended teaching circles; and clerics could be found occasionally on the battlefield.

Significantly, clerics were part of the designating group of notables who gave formal allegiance to a new ruler and acclaimed his accession. Ibn Ghannam makes a point of describing the *shaykh* as the first among all the townspeople and bedouin from across Saudi dominions to give allegiance to ʿAbd al-ʿAziz in 1765 (Ibn Ghannam, 1949, 2:74). According to Ibn Bishr he also ordered the oath of allegiance to Saʿud, ʿAbd al-ʿAziz's son, as heir apparent in 1787/8, albeit with the consent of ʿAbd al-ʿAziz (Ibn Bishr, 1982–3, 1:162).

IMAMATE

The term *imam* in Islam can be confusing. It means literally the man at the front who leads the congregation in prayer and so represents a paid post or unremunerated role at a local mosque. It also refers to the great figures in Islamic thought, such as the great *imams* who founded the four Sunni schools of law. Wahhabi chronicles and writings sometimes refer to Ibn ʿAbd al-Wahhab as a revered *imam* in this sense (e.g. Ibn Ghannam, 1949, 1:3), though he did not receive this religious honorific in his lifetime (Ibn Qasim, ed., 1996–9, 9:9). In traditional Islamic thought the *imam* of the Muslims means the one who leads the community politically, and the supreme *imam* signifies the caliph.

The final political dispensation in the First Saudi State involved rule by the Saudi *imam*. This is sometimes taken as a defining feature of the Saudi political order throughout the first two Saudi states. However, the Saudi imamate was an early nineteenth-century institution that the chroniclers unhistorically and misleadingly projected back onto the First Saudi State of Ibn ʿAbd al-Wahhab's time. Neither ruler Muhammad ibn Saʿud nor his effective son and successor ʿAbd al-ʿAziz ever formally held the title *imam* in their lifetimes; the two major chroniclers apply it to them posthumously.

We should be wary of such attempts to impose order and structure on arrangements and institutions that developed *ad hoc* in response to internal and external pressures. It was ʿAbd al-ʿAziz's son Saʿud who made himself the first Saudi *imam*. His father and grandfather had been called *amir* (one in charge), a term without religious significance. As we shall see, Sa'ud made no claim to the caliphate.

The occasion and rationale for Sa'ud's assumption of the title of *imam* await further research. The very timing, at least ten years after Ibn 'Abd al-Wahhab's death, excludes any direct role by him in founding the institution of the Saudi imamate that survived until the early twentieth century. Ibn 'Abd al-Wahhab failed to supply a conceptual framework for the evolving state, the *raison d'être* of which was to implement and defend his regime of godliness. When the Al Sa'ud did establish the imamate, it may have been at their own initiative, albeit with the apparent consent and support of the *shaykh*'s sons and son-in-law at the top of the religious hierarchy.

We can deduce that, in the absence of a unified Islamic government as conventionally enshrined in the caliphate or supreme imamate, Ibn 'Abd al-Wahhab saw little value in seeking to prescribe the proper form for Islamic government. The ruler needed only to enforce *tawhid* and the *shari'a* as part of a regime of godliness. Had Ibn 'Abd al-Wahhab wished to determine the conceptual and institutional structure of a new state, he could have done, given his influence in al-Dir'iyya and his closeness to ruler 'Abd al-'Aziz. He seems to have chosen not to do so.

ADMINISTRATION OF JUSTICE

Ibn 'Abd al-Wahhab took a close interest in the administration of justice. He was responsible for appointing judges or confirming them in office. Accordingly, he was careful in the first decades to control the treasury which funded both judges and proselytizers. This was important because judges generally served also as *mufti*s, sometimes as *imam*s and preachers at mosques, and even as teachers.

It is not clear how many judges operated at any one time in the heyday of the First Saudi State. The growth in numbers, fueled by heavy investment in Wahhabi religious training, probably kept pace with the expansion of population and governmental responsibilities in conquered territories. In applying justice judges relied on the conservative juridical tradition and the manuals of *fiqh* long established in Najd and based on Ibn Qudama's works. These were so systematizing and codifying that they came to represent juristic orthodoxy in the Hanbali school. These manuals included derivative works of which Ibn 'Abd al-Wahhab disapproved. They remained influential even after the Saudi conquest of the Hijaz in 1924–6. Wahhabism thus brought little change to the basis on which judges made their decisions.

The funding of judges and other clerics was a key issue for Ibn 'Abd al-Wahhab. Some clerics in what he termed the "era of ignorance" had profited from popular festivals and superstitions, as well as from trade and agriculture. He had a notorious row with one opponent who regarded it as acceptable for judges to secure their livelihoods by taking payments from the parties for deciding disputes, so long as this did not lead them to invalidate right or promote wrong. Ibn 'Abd al-Wahhab contended that any payment to deliver a ruling to which the claimant was entitled was a bribe and so prohibited. Gifts to a judge undermined the *shari'a* (Ibn Ghannam, 1949, 1:113, 184, 186–7). He was caustic about the way some clerics sponged off the people by levying redundant retainers for which they delivered no service (ibid., 1:187).

Funding from the Saudi treasury, which relied on efficient and timely collection of alms, put an end to such practices. It enabled, if it did not always deliver, application of the *shari'a* without fear or favor. Equality before the law and in the commanding of right and forbidding of wrong, with enforcement against strong and weak alike, was the proud boast of Saudi chroniclers (Ibn Bishr, 1982–3, 2:376). Saudi rulers sometimes complained of a different reality (e.g. Ibn Qasim, ed., 1996–9, 14:18–25).

SOCIAL JUSTICE

Social justice is not a strong theme in early Wahhabi writings and thought. Ibn 'Abd al-Wahhab associated oppressive rule with the era of ignorance. He and Ibn Ghannam portrayed opposing rulers as naturally oppressive, imposing un-Islamic taxes and brutalizing their subjects (Ibn Ghannam, 1949, 2:3, 6). At least in the early years before the Wahhabis assumed influence in al-Dir'iyya, they were associated as a beleaguered minority with the weak and sometimes derided as poor (ibid., 1:185). Their doctrine of a brotherhood of believers and equality before God was certainly attractive to the disadvantaged and those of low standing in a hierarchical society.

Despite this, Ibn 'Abd al-Wahhab was notoriously distrustful of the populace, fearing popular undercurrents of polytheism and sedition. He focused his attention on the vanguard of true believers and their welfare. Once established in al-Dir'iyya, he worried that political divisiveness would subvert the regime of godliness.

Ibn 'Abd al-Wahhab did criticize various forms of oppression (*zulm*), especially the oppression of polytheism, and sometimes called his clerical opponents oppressors. He claimed they knew only the tyranny of worldly possessions (*zulm al-amwal*) in their eagerness to make money out of their religious activities and in licensing practices forbidden by God, such as charging interest (ibid., 1:148). Yet he did not develop this theme of oppression into a broader concept of social justice. He would have found such a notion hard to square with the principle of absolute obedience to the tyrannical ruler. In the main he showed little apparent interest in social issues.

This did not stop Saudi rulers from 'Abd al-'Aziz onward and the Al al-Shaykh making much in regional epistles of the Wahhabis championing the weak as part of their campaign (see e.g. Ibn Qasim, ed., 1996–9, 1:263). Telling the Ottomans in correspondence that the Wahhabi mission was to act for the weak against the strong, for the oppressed against the oppressor, was a provocative line for the Saudis to take.

CONCLUSION

Social and economic forces probably favored the establishment of political order and the effective management of strained resources in Najd. Yet there was nothing preordained about the rise of Wahhabism and the expansion of the Saudi state. Ibn ʻAbd al-Wahhab was not concerned directly with the formation of a state. His goal was to impose his religious regime on an expanding segment of Najd, for which he required a strong ruler's support. He offered no conceptual or institutional blueprint for government beyond conventional insistence on the need both for the ruler and for total obedience to him.

Ibn ʻAbd al-Wahhab's pragmatic acceptance of small-scale implementation of God's law, and doctrines of association with believers and disassociation with unbelievers, *takfir* and emigration, could perhaps have prompted Wahhabi introspection or disengagement from the wider Najdi community. Had he ever envisaged such a modest outcome for his movement, local and regional opponents ruled it out by inciting rulers to crush the Wahhabis. For the Al Saʻud it became a case of conquer or be conquered. They had to develop the military and financial instruments to ensure their survival. Raw faith, the enmity of their peers, and the predatory interests of clients among both townspeople and nomads propelled them into a rapid territorial expansion that Wahhabi doctrines legitimized.

In developing their state the Al Saʻud benefited greatly from the disciplines the Wahhabi movement imposed on society; its stress on communal solidarity grounded in a brotherhood of believers; its doctrine of obedience; and its investment in religious training and proselytization. Wahhabism helped to externalize traditional Najdi patterns of violence and channeled new-found religious zealotry into *jihad*. It may not have supplied a doctrine of state formation, nor itself constituted a state-building exercise, but it injected an ideology and political glue that enabled a remarkable state to prosper in a fragmented and fissiparous society.

The resulting Saudi state had unbounded territorial ambitions. For many Wahhabis there could be no limits to the territorial claims of their ruler, nor to the regime of godliness that came with Saudi occupation or domination. This outlook brought the Saudis into conflict with the Ottomans. It later subjected the Al Saʻud to domestic pressure from zealots once the former tried to reconfigure the state for new geopolitical realities. On the road to greater pragmatism the Wahhabis learnt some hard lessons.

8

WAHHABISM, SAUDI STATES, AND FOREIGN POWERS

Ibn 'Abd al-Wahhab challenged the authority and status of clerics and opposed religious hierarchies. Yet he himself founded a new Wahhabi hierarchy with a monopoly of religious teaching that until the mid-nineteenth century was little affected by intellectual currents elsewhere in the Islamic world. Students no longer traveled to regional centers other than al-Dir'iyya for instruction. Foreign travel, which exposed students to dangerous influences in heterogeneous environments, became suspect. Such a closed system ill-prepared the Saudis and Wahhabis for their encounters with Ottoman power, Egyptian occupation, British influence, and contending Islamic trends. All of these brought fresh constraints on their ambitions and actions.

One theme runs through the history of the movement to the creation of the modern Saudi Kingdom in 1932 and beyond. It is its struggle to balance ideological purity and political pragmatism in its best long-term interests. Refusal to accommodate changing external realities risked its very existence, especially with the forces of domestic disorder poised to exploit internal weakness or division. Yet senior clerics also wanted to avoid disowning or compromising core beliefs. This chapter outlines how they handled this dilemma until the later twentieth century when fresh ideological influences from outside subjected them and the Wahhabi movement to unprecedented stresses.

SAUDI EXPANSION AND CONQUEST OF THE HOLY CITIES

The Wahhabi cause prospered for two decades after Ibn 'Abd al-Wahhab's death. Hostilities with Sharif Ghalib (d. 1815/16), ruler of Mecca 1787/8–1813, ended temporarily with the Saudis' armed entry into Mecca in 1803. The Ottomans had responded to the *sharif*'s increasingly shrill pleas for help by assaulting Najd from Iraq in 1798–9. They were defeated by the Saudis, who had recently ousted the Bani Khalid, longstanding rulers of al-Ahsa. The Saudis overran Karbala in Iraq in 1802, destroying the tomb of the Prophet's grandson Husayn, beloved of the Shi'a. They besieged Basra twice, without success (Vassiliev, 1998, 93–111).

The first Saudi occupation of Mecca in 1803 was staged by Amir Sa'ud accompanied by Shaykh 'Abd Allah ibn Muhammad ibn 'Abd al-Wahhab. It was followed by a short but thorough Wahhabi campaign to demolish shrines and cupolas (Ibn Bishr, 1982–3, 1:263). The Wahhabis shocked the inhabitants by trying to impose the regime of godliness. They deployed a special group of volunteers to enforce Wahhabi norms, including communal prayers, on pain of death.

These moves and the prior sack of Taif earned the Saudis a reputation for extremism. Further research may show that on occupying the Holy Cities the Wahhabis adapted their doctrines and practices in some respects to a complex and unfamiliar society with varied and mixed religious traditions. They certainly presented their beliefs to local inhabitants in a less uncompromising fashion than hitherto, for instance recognizing as legitimate Sufi orders they saw as observing the *shari'a*.

The Saudis' initial purpose was to extend the regime of godliness to the Hijaz and replenish their coffers for further campaigning, not to impose their sovereignty on the Holy Cities. They left a *sharif* in nominal charge and confirmed the sultan's judges in post. Their initial presence in the Holy Cities was light, and Sharif Ghalib and the Ottomans ousted their first Mecca garrison with ease. The Saudis recovered Mecca in 1806 but throughout their subsequent dominance in the Hijaz their control was limited and uneven. It depended on sympathizers among the sharifian clan. They never took Jidda, base of the Ottoman governor.

Particular awkwardness for the Ottomans came with the annual pilgrimage. The main Ottoman *hajj* caravans threaded their way down from Damascus and Cairo. Commanded by senior Ottoman provincial figures, they had strong military escorts against marauding bedouin. They amounted almost to a yearly Ottoman reconquest of the Hijaz. In a damaging blow to the sultan's prestige the Saudis barred the caravans' entry into the Holy Cities in their traditional format and imposed stringent conditions on pilgrims' progress (Vassiliev, 1998, 105).

The assassination in November 1803 of Saudi ruler 'Abd al-'Aziz at prayers in al-Dir'iyya by an Iraqi, possibly with encouragement from the Ottoman governor of Baghdad, sent relations into a downward spiral. Sharif Ghalib worked hard to poison any prospects of an accommodation between Saudis and Ottomans and to sully the Wahhabis' regional reputation. After a phony war lasting years, an all-out struggle developed between the Ottomans and the Saudis that led to an invasion of the Hijaz by Muhammad 'Ali (d. 1849), the ambitious Ottoman governor of Egypt, at the sultan's insistence in 1811.

SPREADING THE WORD

The Holy Cities gave the Wahhabis a vital platform for spreading their ideology among the thousands of Muslims who converged annually for the pilgrimage. Some may have been discouraged by Saudi actions in blocking the Ottoman pilgrimage caravans with their attendant fanfare or by wild tales of Wahhabi fanaticism. Many others were not, or were unaware of Hijazi developments. The Moroccan caravans proceeded unhindered throughout.

The Saudi *imams* and Wahhabi clerics sent official messages of explanation to regional counterparts with returning caravans, especially along the North African littoral. The Moroccan sultan, who, like his countrymen, was Maliki, was especially receptive. Driven partly by dislike of Sufi political power, he waged his own domestic campaign against manifestations of organized Sufism and saint worship. Clerics in Tripoli and Tunis were less impressed. Two senior Wahhabi clerics (not from the Al al-Shaykh) visited Cairo in 1815 during an armistice. They surprised the *shaykh*s of al-Azhar and the famous Egyptian historian al-Jabarti with their dignity and depth of learning (al-Jabarti, 1958–67, 7:318–19). These were hardly the unlettered nomads Cairenes had expected.

Believing as much in the authority of text as in the edge of the sword, Ibn 'Abd al-Wahhab had created an industry of Wahhabi proselytization. The Wahhabis made compilations of his writings which they distributed widely. Despite powerful early critiques anti-Wahhabis were less meticulous in maintaining their output. The Wahhabis also collected libraries of Islamic and historical works of which they approved. They were accused of widespread bookburning, especially when sacking towns (Dahlan, 1887/8, 230). They denied this but seem to have destroyed or seized particular works they did not want used (Ibn Ghannam, 1949, 1:112).

In peninsular areas beyond direct Saudi control Wahhabi proselytizers targeted communities, sometimes supported by Saudi raiding parties. They often left a contentious legacy, especially where local Sufism was strong, as in the Hadramawt. They were sometimes accused by locals of slaughtering those who resisted. Saudi forces launched concerted assaults on regional concentrations of anti-Wahhabi clerics, many of them Hanbalis, based in al-Zubayr close to Basra and at al-Zubara, a prosperous port on the north side of the Qatar peninsula founded in 1766 that the Saudis attacked in 1795 and occupied in 1809/10 (Ibn Bishr, 1982–3, 1:211, 306–7).

Some of these anti-Wahhabi clerics, who defended the more tolerant, hybrid religious culture of the Gulf with its mixed religious communities, had withdrawn from al-Ahsa as the Wahhabis moved in. Driven out again from al-Zubara, many retreated to Iraq. Clerics from towns such as 'Unayza in the al-Qasim region of northern Najd that were most closely bound by trading links to the Gulf and further afield in the Indian Ocean or to Iraq were often the ones most opposed to Wahhabi exclusivism (Commins, 2006, 50–61). In the Hijaz most clerics rode out the Saudi period and welcomed Muhammad 'Ali and the nominal return of Ottoman rule.

Much of the ideological impact of early Wahhabism in more distant parts of the wider Islamic world came from the ill-documented impact on home communities of returning pilgrims or students who experienced Wahhabi occupation of the Holy Cities. Opinions were doubtless mixed. Some visitors told their communities of their horror at the destruction of beloved shrines and restrictions on traditional rituals of worship. Others passed on the bracing but disruptive message of Wahhabi reform. In this way Wahhabi ideas, often half-digested and distorted, reached dispersed Islamic communities, prompting local discussion, even dissension, and leaving a legacy for later Wahhabis to exploit. More work on Wahhabi influence on Islamic reform movements in Asia and elsewhere would be valuable. Too often commentators have wielded the label "Wahhabi" indiscriminately.

DESTRUCTION OF AL-DIR'IYYA

Egyptian military forces made an uneven start in 1811. They crossed the Red Sea and took Mecca, installing a new *sharif*. They suffered defeats at Saudi hands. As they moved out of the Hijaz and pushed into central Arabia, they were at risk from over-extended lines of communication and supply. In 1816 Muhammad 'Ali gave command to his ruthless son Ibrahim (d. 1848), a military commander of experience and talent. He finally broke into the Saudi heartland and besieged al-Dir'iyya for months in 1818.

After extended battering the Saudi capital capitulated and all Saudi resistance collapsed (Vassiliev, 1998, 151–5). To the dismay of chronicler Ibn Bishr, so too did the regime of godliness and the "community system" he extolled. Najdi turned on Najdi, townspeople and bedouin were once more at odds, and informers were rife (Ibn Bishr, 1982–3, 1:426–7, 2:17). As old ruling families reasserted themselves and the bedouin reverted to type, it must have felt in many places as if Wahhabism and Saudi rule had never existed.

The Egyptians rounded up those Al Sa'ud and clerics they could find and in 1819–21 transported them in batches to Cairo. There many eked out their days in exile. The captive Imam 'Abd Allah was paraded in Cairo by a triumphant Muhammad 'Ali. After a short interval he was transported to Istanbul where he was questioned and executed in December 1818. Observers in both Cairo and Istanbul recorded his composure, straightforwardness, and courage as he prepared to meet his fate (al-Jabarti, 1958–67, 7:447; Burdett, ed., 2013, 1:552).

The Ottoman Sultan Mahmud II (1808–39) relished the triumph and restoration of Ottoman sovereignty in the Holy Cities that was so vital for his regional prestige. But the problem of his expansionist and overmighty subject, Muhammad 'Ali, plagued him for the rest of his days. It took British support and the Convention of London in 1840 to remove Egyptian forces from Syria and Palestine, which they had occupied since 1831, and finally from the Hijaz and inland Arabia.

WAHHABI VIEW OF THE OTTOMANS

In the mid-eighteenth century it was the practice in Najdi mosques for the Ottoman sultan to be praised in the Friday sermon (Ibn Ghannam, 1949, 1:112–13). Lying behind this appears to have been a conventional belief in his leadership of Sunni Islam. Some Najdis may have felt that, however nominally, they were his subjects, despite lying well beyond the reach of Ottoman power or worthwhile territorial ambition. In preceding centuries the Hijazi *sharif*s had raided into Najd but the Ottomans had withdrawn from al-Ahsa in 1670 and were in no position to exercise sovereignty there or in central Arabia. Some local and regional critics labeled the Wahhabis rebels against the sultan. This did not necessarily indicate they were his subjects.

Local critics inferred Ibn 'Abd al-Wahhab's rejection of this conventional outlook from his insistence that the Ottoman sultan not be lauded in the mosque (ibid., 1:132). Hijazis and others likewise assumed Wahhabi repudiation of Ottoman suzerainty over the Holy Cities when the Saudis forbade mention of the sultan in the Friday sermon at Mecca after Sa'ud occupied it in 1803. One Ottoman commander, to stir up anti-Wahhabi sentiment, alleged that Sa'ud had inserted his own name instead ('Abd al-Rahim, 1999, 386). The deletion was, however, on theological or doctrinal grounds and not directed at the legitimacy of Ottoman rule; it remains Wahhabi doctrine and practice to this day to exclude the name of the Saudi ruler from the Friday sermon (al-Fahad, 2004a, 494, n. 22).

In the movement's first decades the Wahhabis were circumspect in offering a view on the Ottomans. Ibn 'Abd al-Wahhab did not mention them in letters to the *sharif*s of Mecca or Hijazi clerics, as recipients must have noticed. Nor did he acknowledge the Ottoman caliphate. The Ottomans asserted this status only after territorial losses to the Russians in the 1770s. They sought to compensate for growing political and military debilitation by claiming spiritual ascendancy over Muslims everywhere.

Claims that in defying the sultan the Saudi *imam* intended to supplant the caliph were unfounded. Classical Wahhabism never accepted the need for a universal caliphate, let alone advocated it or claimed it on behalf of the Saudis or the Arabs more generally. It was part of established Sunni thought that the legitimacy of the caliphate derived from enforcement of the *shari'a*. In his repudiation of the theological stance of the Ottomans and his uninhibited criticism of religious conditions in Ottoman provinces, Ibn 'Abd al-Wahhab made it plain that God's law remained unenforced there. He declined overtly to declare the illegitimacy of Ottoman rule, however implicit this view was in the early Wahhabis designating themselves "the Muslims". We may surmise this was due to political prudence and fear that Wahhabism's initial appeal would be dented by a gratuitous challenge to the Ottomans. It was obvious enough that the Saudis offered an antithetical religious and political model to that of the Ottomans and claimed Islamic leadership on a different basis.

An exception to Ibn 'Abd al-Wahhab's apparent caution is an unusual letter he wrote to a Syrian bedouin *shaykh*. Confident that any self-respecting Syrian cleric would agree privately with his views, he declared that no such Syrian could practise or aver the true religion publicly in Syria for fear the Ottomans would be unhappy. Ibn 'Abd al-Wahhab was fortunate to have a local ruler who followed the truth. The only Syrian who could make public show of that truth would be one at war with the Ottomans. If this was anti-Ottoman incitement, it was couched obliquely. Ibn 'Abd al-Wahhab insisted that his view should remain between himself and his correspondent (Ibn Ghannam, 1949, 1:151–2).

The Saudi relationship with the Ottomans ended in a fight to the death for the Saudi state. It merits more research to track its deterioration. Political confrontation, disputes over Saudi handling of the pilgrimage, and outright conflict led to Wahhabi *takfir* of the Ottomans many years after Ibn 'Abd al-Wahhab's death. Contemptuous propaganda from the increasingly exasperated and worried Ottomans had placed the Wahhabis beyond the religious pale some years before. The Sublime Porte was beset by other problems during the Napoleonic War and embarrassed by losing the Holy Cities. This did not prevent it seeking to buy time by showing apparent readiness to negotiate its way out of a damaging confrontation with the Saudis. A clash that now appears ideologically predetermined and inevitable was a response to changing political circumstance. Mutual antipathy, arrogance, and fear drove both Ottomans and Saudis to ever more extreme positions and ruthless expedients.

Hostility intensified with mutual exchanges of *takfir*. The enmity between Wahhabis and Ottomans became ingrained. Later Wahhabis accused the invading soldiery of polytheism, sodomy, adultery, consumption of alcohol, and missing prayers. The Ottomans never forgave the Wahhabis their conduct in the Holy Cities when they banned the pilgrimage, demolished shrines, disposed of treasures from the Prophet's tomb, and stripped libraries. The antipathy remained until the Ottoman empire collapsed after the First World War. Until then Istanbul claimed suzerainty in Najd. The Saudis, even when driven grudgingly to acknowledge their subordinate status, continued to regard the Ottomans as unbelievers, despite challenges from clerics in al-Qasim and Iraq to this Wahhabi establishment view.

SAUDIS AND CHRISTIAN POWERS

From the turn of the nineteenth century the Saudis began encountering regional manifestations of English and French power. The two European rivals were weighing how this new peninsular power might affect their competition for imperial dominance in India and the Indian Ocean. Curiosity stimulated the first English and French analyses of the Wahhabi movement. Some political officers produced remarkably accurate synopses of the Wahhabis' beliefs while purveying hearsay about their history. Nothing supports the claim that the Wahhabis were incited and supported by the British to rebel against the Ottomans (Abou El Fadl, 2007, 52–3).

Ibn 'Abd al-Wahhab concerned himself little with non-Muslims in his writings, unsurprisingly since the religious status of the Christian *Ifranj* (as Arab Muslims then called the Europeans) was undisputed. The European powers barely impinged directly on the core of the Middle East during his formative years. There were no local Christian or Jewish minorities in the Peninsula to arouse suspicion as potential agents of European powers. Ibn 'Abd al-Wahhab's attention and venom were reserved first for enemies within his own religious and cultural tradition, then for fellow Muslims of different backgrounds.

When Ibn 'Abd al-Wahhab's works refer to Christians it is usually in the doctrinal context of polytheism. They feature as, by definition, further along the spectrum of unbelief than fellow Muslims, rather than as contemporary English or French protagonists. Yet he viewed Jews and Christians as less guilty of rebellion against God than polytheists and apostates who had once known *tawhid*. The latter were worse as they had deliberately perverted their religious inheritance. The Jews and the Christians knew no better. They were People of the Book and derived rights from payment of the *jizya* "head tax." A polytheist held no such status (Rida, ed., 1999, 179). Ibn 'Abd al-Wahhab often praised the asceticism and piety of Christians, however misguided their polytheistic worship of Jesus (Ibn Ghannam, 1949, 1:177).

Napoleon's invasion of Egypt seemed to many Muslims to herald a Christian descent on the Holy Cities. It led in 1798 to some Hijazi elements launching an anti-French *jihad* across the Red Sea. The real threat to the Holy Cities came from the Saudis. Their resolve to pursue their insurgency campaign against the increasingly desperate *sharif* was neither weakened nor deflected by the English and French challenge to

Ottoman rule. That struck critics as opportunistic. The Wahhabis were sapping the strength of the Islamic community just as it came under greatest military, naval, and commercial threat from the Christians. This was an issue Saudis and Wahhabis never acknowledged.

Other Muslims found it hard to understand or forgive the greater hostility the Wahhabis showed toward them than toward Christians. Correspondingly early Wahhabis, including ruler 'Abd al-'Aziz, complained bitterly that their opponents treated them worse than Christians or Jews (Ibn Sihman, ed., 1925/6, 10). One anti-Wahhabi, writing after Napoleon's invasion of Egypt, described *jihad* against the Wahhabis as greater and more meritorious than *jihad* against non-Muslim unbelievers as the danger from the latter was less (al-Haddad, 2005, 125). He also recorded a cleric declaring secondary *takfir* in relation to the Wahhabis, excommunicating not just Wahhabis for their unbelief but anyone who refused to designate them unbelievers (ibid., 22).

The Saudis dealt pragmatically with representatives of the European powers, apparently unconcerned by their unbelief. Their first dealings with the British, and to a lesser extent the French, came during the war with the Egyptians when their priority was to secure their Gulf flank. Their rapid expansion along the Gulf and disruptive impact had threatened Britain's policy, run and supported by the East India Company through their locally based representatives, of preserving the maritime peace while trying to avoid inland entanglements (Burdett, ed., 2013, 1:7). The Saudis upset prevailing arrangements by exploiting rivalries within ruling families. Lacking a navy themselves, they employed the naval power of the Qawasim based around Ras al-Khayma for privateering. This alarmed the British who were ill-placed to tackle an inland power.

The British were keen to reach an accommodation with the Saudis. They assured them that Wahhabi disputes with other Muslims did not interest them. Their priority was peaceful conduct of trade in the Gulf (ibid., 1:72). The Saudi approach was likewise uncolored by religious considerations. In 1810 Imam Sa'ud put out feelers for a treaty with the British. When this did not materialize and he came under Egyptian military pressure from the Hijaz, he tried again in 1813–14 (ibid., 1:73). The British, who stayed neutral in the Ottoman–Saudi conflict and refused naval assistance to Muhammad 'Ali, saw the Saudi star fading and prevaricated until al-Dir'iyya fell.

Nineteenth-century Western commentators were eager to identify Wahhabism with anti-colonial movements, often with little justification. There were so-called Wahhabi trials in Bengal in the 1860s–70s, when Indian Muslims were detained by the authorities of British India and charged with sedition. Then, and later in other circumstances in Asia, the label "Wahhabi" became a pejorative shorthand for religious extremist, however tenuous or non-existent the link between the local religious or political movement and Arabian Wahhabism.

Throughout its history Saudi Wahhabism was broadly free of specifically anti-colonial sentiment or ideology, even if its drive to exclude outside cultural influences made it xenophobic. Even when expansionary Wahhabi tribal elements ran up against colonial borders enforced by the British in Iraq, Jordan, and the Gulf in the 1920s and 1930s, state Wahhabism stood aside in general from the nationalist, anti-colonial (and secular) mood that gripped much of the rest of the Arab world.

THE SECOND SAUDI STATE'S UNEVEN CAREER

After the destruction of al-Dir'iyya had decapitated the Al Sa'ud and dispersed the religious establishment, it took years for Saudi rule to stutter back to life in Najd and for the Al al-Shaykh to recover their position. It was a cadet line of the Al Sa'ud that restored the dynasty and from 1824 reestablished some Saudi control in Najd from a new capital in Riyadh. Turki bin 'Abd Allah (d. 1834) had to compete with rivals and manage the Egyptians, who did not withdraw completely from the Peninsula until 1840–1 (Vassiliev, 1998, 162–73).

After Imam Turki was killed by an Al Sa'ud cousin, other competitors for power emerged. They did not last long. Finally Turki's son Faysal (d. 1865) escaped from Cairo and made himself *imam*. He was returned to Egypt in 1838, only to escape again in 1843 and recover power (Ibn Bishr, 1982–3, 2:63, 207–14). Soon he was sufficiently dominant in Najd to push Saudi influence back into the Gulf. He revived territorial claims he saw as ancestral, citing in evidence of sovereignty old exchanges of correspondence or payments of alms (*zakat*).

To the anxiety of Gulf rulers and the dismay of the British it appeared the Saudis were again a power to fear. Yet, for all its reassertion of territorial claims, over the seventy years of its precarious existence the Second Saudi State exerted much less political and ideological influence beyond central Arabia than its predecessor. It was as if al-Dir'iyya's demise had clouded the self-belief and ambition of the Wahhabi movement. It lacked the same spirit of manifest destiny and became provincial and introverted, concerned more with self-preservation than the wider renewal of Islam.

During the war against the Egyptians Wahhabi clerics had struggled to explain why, if Ibn 'Abd al-Wahhab's doctrines were right and guaranteed worldly success, the Saudis were losing and the regime of godliness was crumbling. They were inclined to blame the sins of the people (ibid., 1:277). The sheer irreligion in Wahhabi eyes of the victorious Egyptian army did not detract from this interpretation. Rather it sharpened the Wahhabi sense of bitterness at a destiny disrupted, if not betrayed. Clerics from al-Qasim had a more cosmopolitan outlook than southern Najdi counterparts and considered the Wahhabi establishment had been too extreme and alienated both the population and God's support (al-Fahad, 2004a, 505–7). The Al al-Shaykh accused these critics of having collaborated with the Egyptians and of being soft on the Ottomans (ibid., 496–7).

There was a question mark, once Imam Turki had installed himself in Riyadh, whether the Al al-Shaykh should resume their leadership of the religious establishment (Rida, ed., 1928, 4:303–4). The leading survivors among clerics from the al-Dir'iyya era were in favor. A grandson of Ibn 'Abd al-Wahhab, 'Abd al-Rahman ibn Hasan (d. 1869), became chief *mufti* after his escape from Egyptian captivity (Ibn Bishr, 1982–3, 2:41–2). The partnership between Saudi *imam* and Wahhabi clerics under the Al al-Shaykh was restored.

Gradually Wahhabi judges and proselytizers fanned back out into Najd and worked to reestablish the regime of godliness that had disintegrated after the fall of al-Dir'iyya. Their style was now less aggressive and their doctrine less exclusivist. The experience of the demolition of the First Saudi State and the exposure of senior Al al-Shaykh to other strands of Islamic scholarship and thinking at al-Azhar, the great Islamic teaching center in Cairo, had mellowed that sense of exceptionalism exhibited and treasured by earlier Wahhabis. Some aspects of Wahhabi doctrine shifted back toward the Sunni mainstream, even as Islamic judges in Najd ruled on the unbelief of the Ottomans in local legal cases (e.g. Rida, ed., 1928, 2(3):232–5).

CIVIL WAR AND COLLAPSE OF THE SECOND SAUDI STATE

The apogee of the Second Saudi State was reached in the last years of Imam Faysal with the Saudi push in the Gulf. It was followed by a devastating period of disintegration, caused by the self-destructive and opportunistic conduct of his four sons. Imam 'Abd Allah (d. 1889) succeeded Faysal in 1865 but by 1866/7 had alienated enough notables for his younger brother Sa'ud (d. 1875) to rebel and dislodge him from Riyadh in 1871. The two alternated as rulers for some years. Seven changes of power in Riyadh took place in the next five years. 'Abd al-Latif (d. 1876), the son of 'Abd al-Rahman ibn Hasan and his successor as chief *mufti*, was in an impossible position. Relying on the traditional Wahhabi requirement for an *imam*, he adopted a flexible stance and accepted each change as it happened (Crawford, 1982).

The situation deteriorated for the Wahhabis when the desperate 'Abd Allah appealed for help to the Ottomans (ibid., 236–7). They had maintained a claim to sovereignty in Najd based on the sultan's role as Muhammad 'Ali's (nominal) overlord. In their view Imam Faysal had been the Ottoman representative in Najd, a status he sometimes acknowledged (Burdett, ed., 2013, 1:81). The Ottomans did little to assert this claim until a senior British representative visited Riyadh in 1865. It looked as if the British were strengthening their hold on the Gulf (ibid., 1:xv). A forward policy by the famous Ottoman reformist governor of Baghdad, Midhat Pasha, led in 1871 to a successful expedition to capture al-Ahsa. This gave the Ottomans control of Najd's access to the sea.

Imam 'Abd Allah's appeal for help was timely for the Ottomans but disastrous for the Wahhabi cause. It horrified Wahhabi establishment clerics, exacerbated disputes with clerics to the north, and discredited the movement (Crawford, 1982, 237–9). Soon a rival dynasty, the Ibn Rashid of Hail in north-western Najd, who had their power base in the large Shammar tribal confederation and were closely linked to the Ottomans, overthrew the tattered Saudi regime and installed a Rashidi governor in Riyadh. The Second Saudi State was extinguished, the youngest surviving brother 'Abd al-Rahman ibn Faysal (d. 1928) was in exile on an Ottoman stipend, and Saudi Wahhabism seemed to have expired, to the relief of most Gulf rulers, the British, Persians, and Ottomans.

RESTORATION AND RENEWAL

It was 'Abd al-Rahman's son, 'Abd al-'Aziz (known as Ibn Sa'ud) (d. 1953), who seized Riyadh in 1902 and restored the fortunes of the Al Sa'ud. He is justly revered as the founder of the modern Kingdom. Many times in succeeding decades the country's fate hinged on his physical and moral courage, and his political and diplomatic skill.

Ibn Sa'ud's ultimate objective as ruler was to recover his patrimonial domains. Drawing initially on the support and advice of Shaykh Mubarak (the Great) of Kuwait (d. 1915), he maneuvered adroitly with the British to secure his position and to outflank the Ottomans and the Ibn Rashid of Hail, from whom he wrestled control of al-Qasim in 1906. By 1913 he had forced Ottoman withdrawal from al-Ahsa while the Ibn Rashid self-destructed with a series of fratricidal killings (Vassiliev, 1998, 210–34).

Ibn Sa'ud tried to draw the British into a treaty putting him on a par with other Gulf rulers under British protection. To the dismay of officials posted into the region from British India, the British Foreign Secretary clung to a pro-Ottoman policy and vetoed any arrangements that would upset the sultan (Burdett, ed., 2013, 1:xvi). This drove Ibn Saʻud into an ill-timed treaty with the Ottomans in May 1914. The outbreak of war aligned the Ibn Rashid with the Ottomans. Those British reporting to London courted Sharif Husain of the Hijaz while British Indian officials conspired to involve Ibn Saʻud against the Ottomans as well as against the Ibn Rashid (Burdett, ed., 2013, 1:xix–xx). The rivalry between Husayn, who anointed himself king of the Arab country in 1916 and claimed the caliphate in March 1924, and Ibn Saʻud intensified, but the latter's subjugation of the debilitated Ibn Rashid in 1921 sealed the fate of Hashimite rule in the Hijaz.

Once Ibn Saʻud had recovered the Holy Cities for Wahhabism in 1924–5, the Islamic world reacted with alarm to Wahhabi destruction of beloved tombs and shrines, imposition of the regime of godliness, and refusal to let the Egyptian pilgrimage caravan arrive to traditional fanfare. There were now no Ottomans to contest Saudi occupation. Attempts by India-based Muslims to internationalize the Hijaz soon fizzled out, as did plots to oust the Saudis from western Arabia after 1932. The Saudis were there to stay, although decades passed before oil revenues allowed them to improve pilgrimage facilities and gain broad acceptance of their suzerainty of the Holy Cities.

With the Saudi return to the Holy Cities, all the old anti-Wahhabi polemics revived. The Saudis showed more sensitivity this time to Islamic opinion and secured backing from some religious reformist intellectuals in Egypt, Iraq, and elsewhere (Laoust, 1939, 533–9). The great Islamic reformer Rashid Rida, in particular, tried to compensate for the stylistic inaccessibility of Ibn ʻAbd al-Wahhab's writings by popularizing and championing Wahhabi ideas in the 1920s–30s. It helped that some leading Wahhabi clerics were well traveled, having taken advantage of the interregnum in Riyadh before 1902 to travel and learn first-hand about different Islamic traditions of learning and activism (Mouline, 2011, 122–4). Ibn Saʻud was keen to reintegrate Wahhabism into the Sunni mainstream and banned the term "Wahhabism" in favor of "Salafism," although worried senior clerics would not countenance dilution of their prerogatives or dogma (ibid., 147, 149, 328).

THE IKHWAN AND INTERNAL DISSIDENCE

We have no record of ideological dissidence within the Wahhabi movement during the First Saudi State. As it expanded, the unruly and brutal activities of some Wahhabi adherents troubled clerics in Riyadh but they presented a reputational risk, not a doctrinal threat. Most nineteenth-century anti-Wahhabism came from regional enemies like Shafi'i *mufti* Dahlan (d. 1886) in Mecca or clerics based in al-Qasim and Iraq (especially al-Zubayr, where anti-Wahhabi Najdis had settled). These disliked the traditional exclusivist outlook of Wahhabi clerics from southern Najd and their anathematizing of the Ottomans and trade with Ottoman-ruled areas.

These critics were the heirs to the original anti-Wahhabis. Disturbingly for Wahhabis some had previously appeared to be part of, or on the fringes of, the Wahhabi establishment. This unnerved Wahhabi clerical champions of the often beleaguered Second Saudi State. They developed an enclave outlook in trying to repel contamination from outside. Conquest of the Holy Cities in 1924–5 inevitably exposed the revived Saudi state to new influences. This forced Najdis to accommodate different Hijazi religious and legal traditions. They had to address institutional and organizational requirements imposed by the Hijaz's greater political sophistication, the challenges of the annual pilgrimage, and international Islamic concerns about it resting in Saudi hands. Ironically against this background, the greatest ideological and military threat was to come from within the once monolithic Wahhabi movement.

One of Ibn Sa'ud's early moves had been to found settlements (each known as *hijra*, pl. *hujar*, signifying place of emigration) to attract bedouin, turn them into agriculturalists, break down tribal bonds, and make them more susceptible to government control. From 1912 tens of settlements were established. Here these bedouin received religious indoctrination along traditional exclusivist lines, fulfilling a longstanding Wahhabi ambition to turn them into proper Muslims. These Ikhwan, as they became known, formed the military vanguard for the campaigns against Hail and the Hijaz.

Once these conquests were complete in 1926, Ibn Sa'ud insisted the Ikhwan stand down to prevent raids beyond Saudi territory triggering war with UK-supported neighbors. Some Ikhwan had already caused trouble through recidivism, insubordination, an excess of zeal in commanding right and preventing wrong, and demands for forced conversion of the Shi'a. Many Ikhwan obeyed the instruction to desist. Others among these indoctrinated but poorly educated proponents of traditional Wahhabism repudiated the international order and the very idea of the Wahhabi state being a territorial state like any other. In their eyes Ibn Sa'ud had forbidden tribal raiding. Now, impermissibly, he was outlawing raiding and plunder against unbelievers beyond Saudi dominions.

This death knell for old-style warfare drove some tribal leaders into a rebellion that Ibn Sa'ud crushed militarily at Sibila in March 1929. The episode left a legacy of tribal bitterness in increasingly neglected *hujar*. It was also a harbinger of trouble decades later. The diehards declared that Ibn Sa'ud had put his relationship with the British unbelievers before his duty to God and Islam, and that the religious establishment had sold out to political power. They expressed their political and social grievances in religious terms, claiming the right themselves to declare offensive *jihad* and challenging the right of senior clerics alone to interpret Wahhabi doctrines (al-Rasheed, 2002, 65–71; Mouline, 2011, 132–42). They were the forerunners of others with different grievances and more developed political and ideological views.

SENIOR CLERICS BECOME OFFICIALS

The Ikhwan extremists attracted minimal support among senior clerics. These stood by Ibn Sa'ud and rejected the notion of freelance *jihad* while reasserting their own prerogatives. He still endured an awkward period with them (al-Fahad, 2004a, 512–14). They disapproved of new technologies like the radio and motor car, and sought a tough approach to Hijazi religious practices and forced conversion of the Shi'a. They were uneasy about new diplomatic relationships that breached the principle of disassociation from unbelievers. They sought abolition of regulations not derived from the *shari'a* and worried about their own control of education and the administration of justice. Thanks to his religious learning, commanding personality and dominance within the Al Sa'ud, the ever pragmatic ruler navigated the squalls without sacrificing authority or objectives. But he could never take clerical support for granted.

The senior Najdi clerics continued to dominate the religious establishment after the Kingdom's unification in 1932. In the 1930s and 1940s they found themselves wrestling with how best to preserve their role, status, and influence in a state that accepted the principle of non-*shari'a* regulations and both non-religious and women's education. That they were comparatively well configured to respond to these threats to their traditional monopolies, as well as the dangerous ideological challenge from Nasserism, was due to an impressive program of change launched by Muhammad ibn Ibrahim Al al-Shaykh (d. 1969), head of the religious establishment.

On his own initiative this far-sighted descendant of Ibn 'Abd al-Wahhab created a formal religious hierarchy, awarding himself the formal title of chief *mufti*. This process contrasted with that elsewhere in the Middle East where such hierarchies were imposed by governments nervous of religious influence. In the 1950s and early 1960s he founded clerical structures in the fields of education, *fatwa* production, justice, and the media, with himself at the center of the web (Mouline, 2011, 178–86). This institutionalization of the religious establishment pre-empted the wider government program to establish modern ministries and bureaucracies that brought many Western-educated Saudis of liberal inclination into senior positions. Shaykh Muhammad ibn Ibrahim countered this development by insisting on clerics controlling some of the new institutions, asserting a clerical lien over the law, education, and social policy, and resisting so far as he could government intrusion into the religious field (ibid., 189–91, 194–5).

These moves came at a cost as senior clerics became more and more integrated into government. They no longer appeared publicly as independent intermediaries between government and people as they had previously, for all the traditional collusion there had always been in private between Al Sa'ud and Al al-Shaykh (Lacroix, 2011, 26–9). On Shaykh Muhammad's death in 1969 King Faysal worked to disperse and weaken clerical authority even in the religious sphere, creating a collective clerical leadership in the Board of Senior 'Ulama in 1971. If ever there was a notion that those in authority (*ulu al-amr*) included senior clerics, it was now clear they were coopted and dependent on the Al Sa'ud.

THE NASSERIST CHALLENGE AND THE SAUDI BID FOR ISLAMIC LEADERSHIP

Ibn Sa'ud's major failure as a leader lay in managing the succession. He had long nominated his son Sa'ud to succeed him on his death (in 1953). Sa'ud proved weak, profligate, and unequal to defending the underdeveloped state from the secular Arab nationalist threat presented by Nasser, military leader of newly republican Egypt. As disputes between Sa'ud and Crown Prince Faysal racked government and the Egyptians intervened militarily in Yemen, Saudi Arabia looked increasingly vulnerable to outside subversion and internal discord. Faysal finally ousted Sa'ud. With clerical and Western support he restored stability and confidence in the face of a secular nationalist trend that stayed strong across the Middle East into the early 1970s.

The political tide across the region turned in the later 1970s in favor of religious ideologies. This was partly due to King Faysal's investment in a policy of Islamic solidarity. He founded new global Islamic institutions in the Hijaz to contest secular, nationalist dogmas and in tandem further Salafi beliefs and Saudi interests. The Muslim World League and the World Assembly of Muslim Youth, founded in 1962 and 1972 respectively, proved valuable instruments of Saudi and Wahhabi influence. So too were Islamic educational institutions such as the Islamic University of Medina (founded in 1961), to which the Saudis welcomed foreign students. As its oil revenues grew, Saudi Arabia assumed a new role as leader of the Islamic world and spread Wahhabism actively overseas not only in Islamic countries but in Islamic communities in the West (Commins, 2006, 152–6; al-Rasheed, 2002, 131–4).

With this new influence came greater integration with the rest of that world and higher exposure to new currents of revivalist and jihadist Islamist thought in the Levant and South Asia. Vitally King

Faysal gave refuge in the 1960s to Muslim Brothers fleeing Nasser's persecution in Egypt. He saw them as Islamist allies determined to resist Western cultural influence, although the Muslim Brotherhood's own strategic aim was to assume power within a constitutional system (its founder did not approve of hereditary monarchy). Among newly arrived exiles were some notably intransigent elements, including the brother of the most radical ideologue of the Brothers, Sayyid Qutb (whom Nasser had executed in 1966 after ignoring Faysal's plea for mercy) (Lacroix, 2011, 38–41).

Sayyid Qutb had taken concepts at the center of Ibn 'Abd al-Wahhab's thought, including ignorance (*jalihiyya*), idolatry (*taghut*), *takfir*, and *jihad*, and driven them in a highly political direction to anathematize, and justify violence against, governments that did not uphold the *shari'a*. His highly educated adherents took their place within Saudi educational institutions, injecting exciting and potentially dangerous ideas into the Wahhabi bloodstream. The Muslim Brothers offered a model of political mobilization and organized themselves in the Kingdom into four distinct networks (ibid., 62–73). Meanwhile Saudi Wahhabism exercised countervailing influence on Muslim Brother thinking, as reflected in the doctrines of the Syrian Muhammad Surur (ibid., 69–70, 123–6). Wahhabi and Salafi ideas were now spreading more widely across the Islamic world beyond Saudi political or doctrinal control.

Just at the time the Wahhabi religious establishment was losing its doctrinal hegemony, influence in fields it once dominated, and ostensible independence of government, Wahhabism in Saudi Arabia was becoming infused with new interpretations. Concepts and terms originally deployed by Ibn 'Abd al-Wahhab proved strikingly adaptable. "Hybrid" radicals drew the line between belief and unbelief at new points on the religio-political spectrum.

Less beholden than establishment clerics to princes, doctrinaire Wahhabis challenged both official clerical authority and the legitimacy of the Al Sa'ud. They claimed senior clerics had subordinated the eternal cause of religion to the short-term interests of the ruling dynasty. The old tension between religious universalism and political particularism had reasserted itself in a new form.

9

WAHHABISM AND RELIGIOUS RADICALISM IN SAUDI ARABIA

By the 1970s Saudi Arabia was buffeted by new internal and external threats. Militant Shi'ism after the Khomeinist revolution in Iran in 1979 challenged Saudi stability and the Wahhabi movement's capacity to respond ideologically. More ominous for state Wahhabism was the radicalization of Sunni elements working to unseat discredited secular nationalist regimes elsewhere in the region. Sayyid Qutb showed how ideologues lacking religious credentials could reinterpret traditional Sunni concepts and turn them against regimes. Now the quietist Wahhabi establishment had to confront threatening strands of politicized thought from within Wahhabism. These imperiled its integrity and longer-term future.

Critics noted that, though condemned as an autodidact himself, Ibn 'Abd al-Wahhab had founded a movement with an authoritarian outlook that brooked little criticism. He had challenged the existing religious consensus yet established a narrower, anti-pluralistic system of belief. He insisted the individual Muslim should base himself or herself directly on the Qur'an and the *Sunna* but permitted only one possible interpretation of God's will, the primacy of *tawhid*. He castigated fellow clerics and challenged the status of clerics and religious hierarchies, yet substituted a new, self-referential religious hierarchy. This was headed first by himself, then by his sons followed by a grandson, and then into the mid-twentieth century by further direct descendants. Above all, he had never explained, save in his own terms, how and why he had a monopoly of the truth. If he could cast off the shackles of previous thought and scholarship and revert to the original sources, so could others, even from within the Wahhabi tradition, and produce different answers.

The lack of a Wahhabi concept of social justice, the doctrine of almost unqualified obedience to political power and the ever closer integration of official Wahhabi clerics into government structures left the religious establishment vulnerable to outflanking by radical religious groups and movements. It lacked new thinking on the state or government and was disengaged from contemporary political issues (al-Rasheed, 2007, 47–8, 56–7). It risked becoming subverted, discredited, and marginalized just when the discontent of those worst affected by fluctuating economic conditions was expressing itself mainly in religious terms.

As Saudi Arabia opened up in the 1970s to outside influences with the onset of oil wealth, the arrival of millions of foreign workers, urbanization, and rapid economic development, some of the basic assumptions underlying state Wahhabism were subject to growing challenge. Further developments in the 1980s made it inevitable that the religious establishment would lose doctrinal control. These included the spread of education and the emergence of a new class of religious intellectual from the mid-1980s. Starting with the cassette, new media arrived. These offered platforms for proselytizing other than the pulpits of mosques controlled by official Wahhabism and the state. Today the internet and social networking media are available to a legion of restless autodidacts. Many with scant religious knowledge are driven by a desire for change on Islamist lines and ready to follow – or issue – religious opinions with direct political implications for the distribution and exercise of power in Saudi Arabia.

THE TRAUMA OF JUHAYMAN

These tensions exploded in the first serious case since the Ikhwan in the 1920s of Wahhabi elements spinning out of the movement and challenging the Saudi state. It was on November 20, 1979, the first day of a new century (the fifteenth) in the Islamic calendar. An armed group of 200–300 young tribesmen (including families), some previously pupils of senior Wahhabi *shaykh*s, occupied the Great Mosque in Mecca. They had earlier heralded the arrival of a messiah or *mahdi* in the form of Muhammad ibn 'Abd Allah al-Qahtani, drawing on a Prophetic tradition and old peninsular legend. Mahdism had an insignificant place in traditional Wahhabism. The group's doctrines also had a more mundane political dimension, including rejection of monarchy. This may have stemmed from Muslim Brother influence among both teachers and foreign students at the Islamic University of Medina.

The leader Juhayman al-'Utaybi came of Ikhwan stock and called his group Ikhwan. Perhaps encouraged by disillusioned senior clerics, he condemned suspension of *jihad*, the corruption of the Al Sa'ud, the role of official clerics as subservient puppets of the regime, and Western domination of the Kingdom. In his view, a ruler who did not follow the Qur'an and *Sunna* and made the people do what he wanted did not have to be obeyed (Hegghammer and Lacroix, 2007). Probably ill at ease and under Al Sa'ud pressure, thirty senior clerics issued a *fatwa* authorizing force in the sacred precincts. Juhayman's millenarian group was rooted out after much bloodshed with the help of French special forces. Having recovered the mosque on December 5, the government executed sixty-three Ikhwan survivors, including Juhayman.

Juhayman's original grouping, from which he and his followers splintered, started as an apolitical and pietist Salafi one concerned with commanding right. Institutionalization from 1926 of this practice Kingdom-wide had given the state a monopoly of enforcement and denied a role to unlicensed faithful. This caused friction between a government wanting closer control and pious Wahhabis who viewed constraints on their duty to command right as against the *shari'a*. Some were frustrated by the failure of official enforcement bodies to act against high level corruption and deviation.

This issue proved a trigger for Juhayman and was later to become a major political, social, and cultural grievance for dissident clerics and others. It bubbled up after the US military came to Riyadh's rescue in September 1990 on Saddam's invasion of Kuwait. It arose again after September 11, 2001 when Washington put intense pressure on Riyadh to tackle extremism. The Al Sa'ud found a balance by investing heavily in enforcement structures while taking ever tighter control of their activities. These episodes showed Ibn 'Abd al-Wahhab's foresight in warning of the destabilizing effect of disputes between zealots and *amirs* over enforcing Wahhabi norms.

THE "AWAKENING"

Juhayman's twisted offshoot of Wahhabism seemed a one-off. A collapse in the oil price in the 1980s saw the professional ambitions and social aspirations of many young Saudis blocked (Lacroix, 2011, 129–31). Their frustration with the Saudi system found outlet when Saudi recourse to unbelievers to defend the Kingdom in 1990–1 triggered major dissidence within the Wahhabi system. The decision raised similar issues to Imam 'Abd Allah's appeal to the Ottomans during the civil war of the 1870s, but this time the foreigners were not even nominally Muslim. Senior Wahhabi clerics gave approval in an unconvincing *fatwa* based on a realistic appreciation of the Al Sa'ud's situation and their own (al-Fahad, 2004a, 485–7, 514–15).

In 1990–2 popular clerics (known as the "Awakening" *shaykh*s) and intellectuals of similar mind rejected this momentous *fatwa* in an unprecedented grassroots challenge to the authority of senior Wahhabis. Simultaneously, secular liberal reformists demanded political change and an end to discrimination against minorities and women. Religious elements, which viewed liberal Saudis as the insidious instrument of Western cultural imperialism, countered with their own public petition. They sought institutional reform but with greater Islamicization, a clear breach of Wahhabi quietist doctrine (Commins, 2006, 176–84). Their Memorandum of Advice in September 1992 criticized reliance on foreigners for defense, the Kingdom's pro-Western foreign policy, and royal corruption. Some adopted the Qutbist principle of the unity of divine sovereignty (*tawhid al-hakimiyya*), which prevented clerics remaining silent when rulers violated the *shari'a*. This threw down the gauntlet to both the religious establishment and the Al Sa'ud (Lacroix, 2011, 148, 158–93).

Such an outbreak of politics and open disputation strained the careful division of responsibilities between senior Wahhabi clerics and the Al Sa'ud, already undermined by the latter's tightening grip on the religious sector. This division had traditionally preserved distance in public discourse between religion and politics. It was vital for religious legitimation of Saudi rule. The challenge created a crisis. Wahhabism lacked doctrinal elasticity. It offered no effective channel for political dissent short of rebellion. Even the slightest political activism could be treated as rebellion. Revolt could be justified only if the ruler himself was judged guilty of unbelief and made subject to *takfir* (with the corollary of *jihad*) (al-Rasheed, 2007, 50–4). Neither the "Awakening" movement nor other reformist currents initially called for violence or overthrow of the Al Sa'ud.

The senior Wahhabi cleric 'Abd Allah bin Baz (d. 1999) signed the original petition, thinking it would not be publicized (Mouline, 2011, 311). King Fahd was angry that he was not given private advice in line with Wahhabi precepts. He expelled members of the Board of Senior 'Ulama who refused to retract their signatures on the memorandum. He launched a crackdown that pitted the "Awakening" movement against a divided Wahhabi establishment. The younger *shaykh*s accused the senior official *shaykh*s of losing touch with people's concerns, ignoring threats to Islamic states and communities outside, and focusing too much on public morality and minor details of ritual (Lacroix, 2011, 144–7). Some repudiated the very notion of the Wahhabi religious hierarchy. Especially once Bin Baz died, the innate authority of senior clerics diminished, although the king tried bolstering it with Al al-Shaykh promotions. Official Wahhabism had become one strand of Salafism among others in the Kingdom (al-Rasheed, 2007, 58).

JIHADISM

This is not the place to review influences on the "Awakening" movement. It reflected many different, even mutually hostile, currents (ibid., 66–72). To a degree it paved the way for the emergence of jihadi groups. But the "Awakening" *shaykh*s condemned their violence, declaring it was for the ruler to remove infidels from the Peninsula (ibid., 83–4). Some *shaykh*s helped the regime reclaim jihadis from violence by encouraging recantation. The government gradually muzzled them and excluded them from the political sphere. With politics suppressed, and the Islamic world in turmoil over the 2003 US invasion of Iraq, it was the turn of violent jihadis to contest the Al Sa'ud. They had been a force in the Kingdom even before they made contact with al-Qa'ida in the late 1990s (Lacroix, 2011, 249–55).

The backdrop was the training, arming, and funding by the Saudi government, Muslim World League, Muslim Brothers, and individuals in the Kingdom of enthusiastic young Saudis to wage *jihad* against the Soviets in Afghanistan. A local champion emerged in Usama bin Ladin (d. 2011), founder of al-Qa'ida. He came from a Hadrami family closely associated with the Al Sa'ud and was frustrated at his exclusion from Saudi politics. Unconstrained by Wahhabi clerics or Saudi control, he became radicalized in the Afghanistan–Pakistan borderlands through association with other jihadists, including the leading Muslim Brother 'Abd Allah 'Azzam (d. 1989). He developed a transnational jihadist outlook and network. He concluded that the Saudi king was apostate and declared *jihad* against the Kingdom and the West (Commins, 2006, 184–90). The traditional concepts of dissociation from unbelievers, *takfir* and *jihad* were now wielded against the Wahhabi state itself (al-Rasheed, 2007, 258–9).

Both Bin Ladin and Ayman al-Zawahiri, his lieutenant who emerged from jihadist groups in Egypt, were autodidacts without formal religious training. The ideology they shaped for al-Qa'ida blended Wahhabism, Qutbist thought, and elements from elsewhere, including mysticism. Some components, such as the demand for an Islamic caliphate, had no roots in traditional Wahhabism (see ibid., 117–20, 258). However, once it emerged that nearly all the nineteen hijackers who flew into the Twin Towers in New York on September 11, 2001 were Saudis, it was inevitable that anti-Wahhabis would seek to blame the "virulent" effect of Wahhabi ideology supported by Saudi funding, if not the shocked Saudi regime directly. One author appears to associate Wahhabis with terrorism in the title of a book (Allen, 2006).

The Saudi regime managed to crush the campaign launched in 2003 by young jihadists who could not see why *jihad* overseas was acceptable but violence at home illegitimate. They launched attacks on expatriate compounds, key economic points, US facilities, and individual

Westerners. They drew on the support and sympathy of those similarly radicalized by Afghan experience or dissatisfied with the political and religious status quo. These actions threatened at one point to develop into an insurgency. But the Saudi authorities mobilized their resources and social and religious elements in support. They expelled jihadist remnants into Yemen where they continue to fight under the banner of al-Qa'ida in the Arabian Peninsula (Hegghammer, 2010, 157–226).

This outcome has left the futures of the Wahhabi movement and the Al Sa'ud more secure than they appeared in 2004–5. The underlying issues of political dispensation and religious authority remain unresolved in a country increasingly exposed to outside influence and subject to severe demographic, social, and economic pressures. The spread of education and aspiration among the ever younger population will inevitably generate further demands for change. The Al Sa'ud have never had more need to display their dynastic talent for balancing interests. Nor, for the longer-term interests of the Wahhabi movement, has there been more need for Ibn 'Abd al-Wahhab's descendants and senior clerical heirs to reclaim influence and prestige among Saudis deeply imbued with Wahhabi culture yet increasingly resistant to constraints on their ability to choose their own destinies.

10

IBN 'ABD AL-WAHHAB'S LEGACY

I have tried to show how and why the legacy of Ibn 'Abd al-Wahhab has been so powerful and so disputed. The simplest internet search on Wahhabism throws up results that illustrate its enduring impact. They also reveal Wahhabi manifestations beyond Arabia that this brief book has not mentioned. The story of Wahhabism in all its guises is far from ended. Its future in Arabia may be clouded with uncertainty but it continues to exert strong influence on Islamic communities worldwide.

Ibn 'Abd al-Wahhab serves as a model to emulate for some Muslims. Aspiring Salafis can associate with his divisive campaign to make the Sunni community eradicate the corruption within, to trigger the religion's immune system. He intended the doctrines buttressing the credo of *tawhid* – association with believers, primary and secondary *takfir*, *hijra*, and *jihad* – to draw a sharp line between true believers and others. He wanted to prevent false doctrinal or ideological compromise. He viewed violence as not only justified but necessary to defend the citadel of faith. For critics this was a campaign to fracture the unity of the Sunni community, grounded in thought they considered narrow and shallow and executed with bigotry and intolerance.

Ibn 'Abd al-Wahhab's claim to originality lies not in his key themes. These lack theological or conceptual novelty. It lies in his single-minded focus on *tawhid* and drive as a radical activist to implement his credo through his role as guide to an expansionist Saudi state. The very simplicity of his doctrines has exercised strong intellectual appeal for later generations. His repudiation of religious hierarchies and insistence on the individual's direct access to God have lent Wahhabism a strong flavor of ideological modernity to blend with the aura of cultural authenticity that it draws from being historically a pre-modern phenomenon.

Other ideological elements reinforce Wahhabism's appeal in today's globalized, internet-enabled world. By rejecting esoteric thought and practices and local syncretist additions to the religion, it enables broad standardization of belief and practice. Its insistence on action to establish the regime of godliness, even on a small scale, places value, first, on the collective success of the religious community in this world over the individual's spiritual route to salvation in the next; second, on the vanguard of true believers over the rest of society; and third, on religious allegiance and solidarity over emotional drivers or worldly motives. To those dislocated by social or economic change, these tenets offer a sense of specialness, group identity, and shared mission.

Modern Arabian Wahhabism has exercised influence less under the movement's own label than under the broader rubric of Salafism, which shares these ideological features. Ibn ʿAbd al-Wahhab campaigned against the pluralistic tendency of Islamic consensus to accommodate doctrines or practices within Sunnism that breached his version of *tawhid*. Today's Salafis spearhead Islamist repudiation of any global convergence of values based on Western liberalism.

The modern Salafi landscape is itself politicized and fragmented. Many disparate, contradictory, and even mutually hostile trends have emerged across the Islamic world. By submerging their religious identity, for defensive and offensive purposes, into that of Salafism, Arabian Wahhabis and the Saudis have heightened the risk of global association with extremist and violent Salafi trends like al-Qaʿida. Even though Saudi Arabia has itself been a victim of jihadist and al-Qaʿida terrorism, this linkage has hurt the Wahhabi movement's reputation.

Recent decades in Arabia have exposed once more some of Wahhabism's inherent tensions, especially that between the universalism of its religious message and the particularism of its political attachment to the Al Saʿud dynasty. Both internally and externally, the Saudi connection has been both its greatest strength and the greatest single constraint on its ideological influence thanks to the politically motivated resistance it has aroused. Even modern Islamic radicals who rely on Ibn Taymiyya's theories to help them contest the legitimacy of their regimes tend to disown any debt to Wahhabism just because it is the official creed of the conservative Saudi state.

We have traced the recent emergence of doctrinal dissidence within Saudi Wahhabism. Ibn 'Abd al-Wahhab's original failure – or refusal – to address the crucial issue of how Islamic government should be organized, to limit the principle of political obedience, and to develop thinking on social justice has left the Wahhabi religious establishment at risk of being discredited as the instrument of Al Sa'ud religious legitimation. He supplied the conceptual bases for greater political and legal radicalism but, whether from political pragmatism or limited intellectual curiosity and range, did not pursue or even explore their logic.

Ibn 'Abd al-Wahhab's influence within the self-referential and closed clerical system he founded has been so overwhelming that his successors and descendants have not tested the conceptual boundaries he set. Instead they have subordinated doctrinal purism to the interests of preserving the regime of godliness, as guaranteed by the Al Sa'ud. Their resulting image as a self-serving religious interest group within government has allowed non-state radicals to claim Ibn 'Abd al-Wahhab's doctrinal and ideological legacy. Some denounce senior clerics as having betrayed his heritage (al-Rasheed, 2007, 71, 211).

Rejecting part of the Wahhabi doctrinal and institutional superstructure in their search for unmediated access to the true Salafi path, these radicals have exploited elements within that legacy to challenge the status quo. This recalls the first subversive years of Wahhabism before it became a state dogma. These new hybrid Wahhabis are more politically driven than Ibn 'Abd al-Wahhab ever was but, in an Islamic world afflicted by religious and ideological disturbance and marred by popular frustration at entrenched patterns of power and privilege, he still represents an inspiring example of unrelenting struggle and certitude of faith. Those fighting the prevailing consensus and striving to force the issue of political and religious legitimacy within their own communities take heart from the achievement of someone dedicated enough to denounce the majority, even when isolated and under siege.

Although Ibn 'Abd al-Wahhab waged his reformist campaign on the geographical, political, and social margins of the eighteenth-century Islamic world, it generated waves that washed against its furthest shores within a few years of his death. It is a measure of his impact that the religious, political, and cultural aftershocks reverberate across continents nearly three centuries later.

BIBLIOGRAPHY

This is an alphabetical list of books and articles referred to in the text:

'Abd al-Rahim, 'Abd al-Rahim, *Al-Dawla al-Sa'udiyya al-ula*, Cairo, Dar al-Kitab al-Jami'i, 1999
Abou El Fadl, K., *The Great Theft*, New York, HarperOne, 2007
Abu Hakima, A. (ed.), anonymous *Lam' al-Shihab fi sirat Muhammad ibn 'Abd al-Wahhab*, Beirut, Dar al-Thaqafa, 1967
Algar, H., *Wahhabism: A Critical Essay*, New York, Islamic Publications International, 2002
Allen, C., *God's Terrorists, the Wahhabi Cult and the Hidden Roots of Modern Jihad*, London, Little, Brown, 2006
Axworthy, M., *The Sword of Persia*, London, I.B. Tauris, 2009
Al Bassam, 'Abd Allah, *'Ulama Najd khilala thamaniya qurun*, 6 vols., Riyadh, Dar al-'Asima, 1998/9
Burdett, A. (ed.), *The Expansion of Wahhabi Power in Arabia 1798–1932*, 8 vols., Cambridge, Cambridge University Press, 2013
Commins, D., *The Wahhabi Mission and Saudi Arabia*, London, I.B. Tauris, 2006
Crawford, M., "Civil War, Foreign Intervention, and the Question of Political Legitimacy: A Nineteenth-Century Sa'ūdī Qāḍī's Dilemma," *International Journal of Middle East Studies* 14, 1982, pp. 227–48
——, "The Da'wa of Ibn 'Abd al-Wahhāb before the Al Sa'ūd," *Journal of Arabian Studies* 1(2), 2011, pp. 147–61
Dahlan, Ahmad Zayni, *Khulasat al-Kalam*, Cairo, al-Matba'a al-Khayriyya, 1887/8
al-Dakhil, K., "Wahhabism as an Ideology of State Formation," in Ayoob, M. and Kosebalaban, H., eds, *Religion and Politics in Saudi Arabia: Wahhabism and the State*, Boulder, Lynne Rienner, 2009, pp. 23–38
Dallal, A., "The Origins and Objectives of Islamic Revivalist Thought, 1750–1850," *Journal of the American Oriental Society* 113(3), 1993, pp. 341–59

——, "The origins and early development of Islamic reform" in Hefner, R., ed., *The New Cambridge History of Islam*, Cambridge, Cambridge University Press, 2011, pp. 107–47

Enayat, H., *Modern Islamic Political Thought*, London, Macmillan, 1982

al-Fahad, A., "From Exclusivism to Accommodation: Doctrinal and Legal Evolution of Wahhabism," *New York University Law Review* 79(2), 2004a, pp. 485–519

——, "The *'Imama* vs. the *'Iqal*: Hadari-Bedouin Conflict and the Formation of the Saudi State," in al-Rasheed, M. and Vitalis, R., eds, *Counter-Narratives*, New York, Palgrave Macmillan, 2004b, pp. 35–75

Gibb, H.A.R., *Modern Trends in Islam*, Chicago, University of Chicago Press, 1947

al-Haddad, 'Alawi, *Misbah al-Anam wa-jala' al-zalam*, Istanbul, 2005, downloaded from http://www.hakikatkitabevi.com/arabic/arabic.htm on 15 May 2014

Hegghammer, T., *Jihad in Saudi Arabia*, Cambridge, Cambridge University Press, 2010

Hegghammer, T. and Lacroix, S., "Rejectionist Islamism in Saudi Arabia: The Story of Juhayman al-'Utaybi Revisited," *International Journal of Middle East Studies* 39, 2007, pp. 103–22

Hopwood, D., "The Ideological Basis: Ibn 'Abd al-Wahhab's Muslim Revivalism," in Niblock, T., ed., *State, Society and Economy in Saudi Arabia*, London, Croom Helm, 1982, pp. 23–35

Ibn 'Abd al-Wahhab, Sulayman, *al-Sawa'iq al-Ilahiyya fi al-Radd 'ala al-Wahhabiyya*, Casablanca, al-Multaqa, 2005

Ibn Bishr, 'Uthmān, *'Unwan al-Majd fi tarikh Najd*, 2 vols., Riyadh, Darat al-Malik 'Abd al-'Aziz, 1982–3

Ibn Ghannam, Husayn, *Tarikh Najd al-musamma Rawdat al-Afkar wa-l-afham*, 2 parts, Riyadh, al-Maktabat al-Ahliyya, 1949

Ibn Qasim, 'Abd al-Rahman (ed.), *al-Durar al-Saniyya fi al-ajwiba al-Najdiyya*, 16 vols., Riyadh, n.p., 1996–9

Ibn Sihman, Sulayman (ed.), *al-Hadiyya al-Saniyya wa-l-Tuhfa al-Wahhabiyya*, Cairo, al-Manar, 1925/6

al-Jabarti, 'Abd al-Rahman, *'Aja'ib al-Athar*, 7 vols., Cairo, Lajnat al-Bayan al-'Arabi, 1958–67

Juhany, U., *Najd before the Salafi Reform Movement*, Reading, Ithaca Press, 2002

Lacroix, S., *Awakening Islam*, Cambridge, Mass., Harvard University Press, 2011

Laoust, H., *Essai sur les doctrines sociales et politiques de Takī-d-Dīn Aḥmad b. Taimīya*, Cairo, l'Institut Français d'archéologie orientale, 1939

Margoliouth, D.S., "Wahhābīya," in *Encyclopaedia of Islam*, 1st edn, 8 vols., Leyden, Brill, 1913–38, at vol. 8, pp. 1086–90

Mouline, N., *Les Clercs de l'Islam*, Paris, Presses Universitaires de France, 2011

Nafi, B., "A Teacher of Ibn 'Abd al-Wahhāb: Muḥammad Ḥayāt al-Sindī and the Revival of *Aṣḥāb al-Ḥadīth*'s Methodology," *Islamic Society and Law* 13(2), 2006, pp. 208–41

Nakash, Y., *The Shi'is of Iraq*, Princeton, Princeton University Press, 2003

al-Rasheed, M., *A History of Saudi Arabia*, Cambridge, Cambridge University Press, 2002

——, *Contesting the Saudi State*, Cambridge, Cambridge University Press, 2007

Redissi, Hamadi, *Le Pacte de Nadjd Ou comment l'islam sectaire est devenu l'islam*, Paris, Seuil, 2007

Rida, Rashid (ed.), *Majmu'at al-Tawhid al-Najdiyya*, Riyadh, al-Amana al-'Amma, 1999

—— (ed.), *Majmu'at al-Rasa'il wa-al-Masa'il al-Najdiyya*, 4 vols., Cairo, al-Manar, 1928

al-Rumi, 'Abd al-'Aziz, al-Bultaji, Muhammad, and Hijab, Sayyid (eds), *Mu'allafat al-Shaykh al-Imam Muhammad ibn 'Abd al-Wahhab*, 12 vols., Riyadh, Jam'iat al-Imam Muhammad ibn Sa'ud al-Islamiyya, 1978, including *al-Rasa'il al-Shakhsiyya (RS)*, *al-'Aqida* (2 parts) (*'Aqida*), *al-Fiqh* (*Fiqh*), *Mukhtasar sirat al-Rasul* (*Sira*)

Ruthven, M., *A Fury for God*, London, Granta, 2004

al-Shawkani, Muhammad, *al-Badr al-Tali'*, 2 vols., Cairo, Matba'a al-Sa'ada, 1929/30

Al al-Shaykh, 'Abd al-Rahman ibn Hasan, *al-Maqamat*, Riyadh, Darat al-Malik 'Abd al-'Aziz, 2005

al-Taqwa, Abu al-'Ulla, *al-Firqa al-Wahhabiyya fi khidmat man?* Beirut, al-Irshad li-l-Taba'a wa-l-Nashr, n.d.

Traboulsi, S., "An Early Refutation of Muḥammad ibn 'Abd al-Wahhāb's Reformist Views," *Die Welt des Islams* 42(3), 2002, pp. 373–415

Vassiliev, A., *The History of Saudi Arabia*, London, Saqi Books, 1998

FURTHER READING

Cook, M., "On the Origins of Wahhabism," *Journal of the Royal Asiatic Society* 3(2), 1992, pp. 191–202
——, "The Expansion of the First Saudi State: The Case of Washm," in Bosworth, C., Issawi, C., Savory, R. et al., *The Islamic World*, Princeton, Darwin Press, 1989, pp. 661–99
DeLong-Bas, N., *Wahhabi Islam, From Revival and Reform to Global Jihad*, London, I.B. Tauris, 2004
Determann, J.M., *Historiography in Saudi Arabia*, London, I.B. Tauris, 2014
Habib, J., *Ibn Sa'ud's Warriors of Islam*, Leiden, Brill, 1978
Helms, C., *The Cohesion of Saudi Arabia*, London, Croom Helm, 1981
Peskes, E., *Muḥammad b. 'AbdalWahhāb (1703–92) im Widerstreit*, Beirut, Franz Steiner, 1993
—— with Ende, W., "Wahhābiyya" in Bearman, P., et al., eds, *Encyclopaedia of Islam*, 2nd edn., Brill, Leyden, vol. 11 (2002), pp. 39–47
Philby, H. St. J., *Sa'udi Arabia*, Beirut, Librairie du Liban, 1955
al-Rasheed, M., "The Shia of Saudi Arabia: A Minority in Search of Cultural Authenticity," *British Journal of Middle Eastern Studies* 25(1), 1998, pp. 121–38
Rentz, G., *The Birth of the Islamic Reform Movement in Saudi Arabia*, London, Arabian Publishing, 2004
Sirriyeh, E., "Wahhabis, Unbelievers and the Problems of Exclusivism," *Bulletin (British Society for Middle Eastern Studies)* 16(2), 1989, pp. 123–32
Steinberg, G., *Religion und Staat in Saudi-Arabien: die wahhabitischen Gelehrten 1902–1953*, Würzburg, Ergon, 2002
——, "The Wahhabi Ulama and the Saudi State: 1745 to the Present," in Aarts, P. and Nonneman, G., eds, *Saudi Arabia in the Balance*, New York, New York University Press, 2006, pp. 11–34
Troeller, G., *The Birth of Saudi Arabia*, London, Cass, 1976
al-'Uthaymīn, 'Abd Allāh, *Muḥammad ibn 'Abd al-Wahhāb*, London, I.B. Tauris, 2009
Winder, R.B., *Saudi Arabia in the Nineteenth Century*, London, Macmillan, 1966

INDEX

Note: Page numbers in **bold** type indicate map.

9/11 attacks 10–11, 132

'Abd Allah 'Azzam (d. 1989) 132
'Abd Allah bin Baz (d. 1999) 131
'Abd Allah ibn 'Abd al-Latif (d. 1751/2) 75
'Abd Allah ibn Faysal ibn Turki
   (d. 1889) 119–20, 130
'Abd Allah ibn Muhammad ibn 'Abd
   al-Wahhab (b. 1751/2) 44, 86, 108
'Abd Allah ibn Sa'ud (d. 1818) 86, 99,
   111–12
'Abd Allah al-Mu'ammar (d. 1725/6) 28
'Abd Allah al-Muways (d. 1761/2) 75
'Abd al-Aziz ibn Muhammad ibn Sa'ud
   (d. 1803) 39, 42, 116
   assassination 109
   and Ibn 'Abd al-Wahhab 41, 43, 96,
     101–3
   and saints 84
   and Wahhabism 32, 105
'Abd al-Latif ibn 'Abd al-Rahman ibn Hasan
   (d. 1876) 119
'Abd al-Qadir al-Jilani (d. 1166) 28, 85
'Abd al-Rahman ibn Faysal (d. 1928) 120
'Abd al-Rahman ibn Hasan (d. 1869) 118,
   119
'Abd al-Wahhab ibn Sulayman (d. 1741) 22,
   28–30
Abou El Fadl, K. 11, 77
absolutism, Wahhabi 1, 13, 26, 92
Ahmad ibn 'Ali al-Qabbani 75, 85
Ahmad ibn Hanbal (d. 855) 20, 32, 38, 53
al-Ahsa:
   Ibn 'Abd al-Wahhab in 22, 27, 85

   and opposition to Ibn 'Abd
     al-Wahhab 39, 75, 110
   and Ottoman empire 112, 120
   Saudi occupation 8, 87, 108, 110
Al-Shaykh 100, 101–2, 105, 117–18,
   131
Al Rashid 81, 120, 121
Al Sa'ud:
   and control of Holy Cities 1, 40
   defeats 43, 117
   and Ibn 'Abd al-Wahhab 14–15, 35–8,
     39, 41–4, 46, 69, 73–6, 78, 89
   and influence of Wahhabism 1–2, 8, 16,
     77–8, 106, 133, 136–7
   and radicalism 127–33, 137
   rivals 81
   and Shi'ism 87–8
   and Sufism 86, 108
   transportation to Egypt 111–12, 117
   see also First Saudi State; Holy Cities;
     Saudia Arabia, Kingdom; Second Saudi
     State
'Alawi al-Haddad 75
Algar, H. 49
'Ali ibn 'Abi Talib 86–7
*amir*s:
   appointment 101
   in First Saudi State 103
   obedience to 97–8, 99, 105
'Anaza tribe 79
apostasy 51, 61, 84
   by bedouin 79–80
   by rulers 98–9
   by Wahhabis 42, 59

Arabian Peninsula, map 17
al-'Arid 19, 21, 92
association and disassociation 58–9, 65–6, 67, 71, 106, 123, 132
associationism 55, 87
Awakening 130–1
'Aydarus Sufi order 85
Ayman al-Zawahiri 132
al-Azhar 110, 119

Bani Khalid tribe 27, 32–3, 36, 39, 43, 81, 108
Bani Tamim tribe 20
Basra:
  campaign against polytheism 26
  and First Saudi State 108
  Ibn 'Abd al-Wahhab in 22, 24–5, 27, 49, 57, 85
  and Shi'ism 25–6, 87
bedouin 76–8
  and customary law 78–9
  and First Saudi State (1744–1818) 94
  and *jihad* 70
  and Saudi Kingdom 122
  and *takfir* 79–80, 81
  and tribalism 80–2
  tribute payments 81–2
Bin Ladin, Usama 1, 132
bookburning, accusations 15, 110
Britain:
  control of India 7
  and First Saudi State 114–17
  and Ottoman empire 120–1
  and Saudi Kingdom 120–1, 123
  and Second Saudi State 119–20

caliphate 103, 112, 132
Christianity 84
  and polytheism 115
  and *tawhid* 29, 115
  see also Europe
clerics:
  and Awakening 130–1
  and bedouin 79
  and First Saudi State 100–2, 110
  and Ibn 'Abd al-Wahhab 47–8, 56, 73–6, 80, 128
  as judges 103–4
  Meccan 31

Najdi 21–2, 37–8, 54, 73–7, 90
North African 109–10
  and Saudi Kingdom 123–5, 129, 133
  and Second Saudi State 118–19
  and Sufism 85
community, Islamic (*umma*) 12, 20, 95–6, 97–8, 100, 106
  and individual 83, 136
Companions of the Prophet:
  and Shi'a 86–7
  shrines 24, 32, 57–8
consensus (*ijma'*) 9, 11, 20, 48, 52

Dahham ibn Dawwas (ruler of Riyadh) 40–1, 43
Dahlan, Ahmad ibn Zayni (d. 1886) 122
al-Dakhil, K. 91, 92
Dallal, A. 49
dervishes, opposition to 28, 31, 85
al-Dir'iyya (town) 32, 76
  and Al Sa'ud 39, 89, 91, 117
  Egyptian conquest 86, 111–12, 117–18
  Ibn 'Abd al-Wahhab in 33, 35–42, 66–7, 70, 92, 101
  Najrani siege 43
  and regime of godliness 35, 39, 92
  replacement of *qadi* 39
  and Riyadh 40–1
  and tribalism 80
dissimulation (*taqiyya*) 26, 63, 87
diversity, religious *see* pluralism

ecumenism, Sunni–Shi'i 25–6
egalitarianism 60
Egypt:
  French invasion 5–6, 7, 115–16
  invasion of Najd 82, 86, 100, 111–12, 117–18
  and Saudi Kingdom 121
  see also Nasserism
emigration (*hijra*) 58–9, 66
Enayat, H. 88
England *see* Britain
equality of believers 12, 60, 105, 106
Europe:
  and First Saudi State 114–17
  and Second Saudi State 119–20
exclusivism 9–10, 12, 23, 31, 52, 73, 110, 119, 122

excommunication (*takfir*) 126
  of bedouin 79–80, 81
  of Ibn 'Abd al-Wahhab 39, 70
  by Ibn 'Abd al-Wahhab 31, 58, 61–5, 83–4
  of individuals 61–4
  mass 64
  of Ottomans 114
  secondary 65–9, 71, 116
  of Wahhabis 37, 38, 65, 76, 116
extremism, Islamic 10–11, 52, 117, 129, 131–3, 136

Fahd ibn 'Abd al-'Aziz Al Sa'ud, King (d. 2005) 131
faith (*'aqida*) 49, 53
Faysal ibn 'Abd al-'Aziz Al Sa'ud, King (d. 1975) 124–6
Faysal ibn Turki, Imam (d. 1865) 36, 117–18, 119
First Saudi State (1744–1818) 9, 89–106
  and bedouin 82, 94
  and Christian powers 114–17
  and clerics 100–2
  expansion 108–10, 135
  extent 17
  and imamate 36, 102–3
  and *jihad* 71
  and local *amirs* 97–8, 99, 101
  and obedience to rulers 98–100, 105, 106
  and Ottoman empire 9, 105–9, 111–12, 114–17
  and regime of godliness 92–8, 99, 103, 105–6, 108
  and Shi'a 87–8
  and state formation 89–90, 92–4, 96–8, 103, 106
  and tribute payments 82
France, and First Saudi State 114–17

Ghalib, Sharif (d. 1815/16) 108, 109
godliness, regime 14–15, 69
  in al-Dir'iyya 35, 39, 92, 105
  and First Saudi State 92–8, 99, 103, 105–6, 108
  in Huraymila 28
  and Saudi Kingdom 121, 136, 137
  and Second Saudi State 118–19
  in al-'Uyayna 31–3, 92

governance, Islamic 96–8, 100–2, 103, 106, 126, 137

hadith, in Ibn 'Abd al-Wahhab's writings 49–50
Hamid ibn Nasir (son-in-law of Ibn 'Abd al-Wahhab; d. 1811) 54, 99
Hanafi school of law 23
Hanbali school of law 21, 22, 27, 48, 51–4, 70, 75, 110
  and *jihad* 101
  and jurisprudence 104
  persecution of Hanbalis 38
  and public and private 95
  and quietism 20
  and Shi'a 86
  and Sufism 28, 84, 86
Hashimite sharifs 8, 87, 121
hierarchies:
  religious 12–13, 47–8, 84, 102–3, 107, 124, 127, 131, 135
  social 81
hijra see emigration
Hijaz:
  Ottoman control 112
  and Saudi expansionism 108–10
Holy Cities:
  and First Saudi State 7–8, 40, 86, 98, 108–11, 114, 115–16
  Ibn 'Abd al-Wahhab in 22–4, 27, 31
  and opposition to Ibn 'Abd al-Wahhab 31–2, 74–5
  Ottoman control 5, 7–8, 24, 108–9, 112
  and Saudi Kingdom 9, 121, 122
  and Shi'ism 87
  and Sufism 85, 108
holy men, condemnation 38, 83–5
Hopwood, D. 45
Huraymila, Ibn 'Abd al-Wahhab 28–30, 49, 57–8, 101
Husain ibn 'Ali (Sharif of Hijaz; d. 1931) 121
hypocrites, as fifth column 59–60, 62–3, 82

Ibn 'Abd al-Wahhab, Muhammad:
  as activist 1, 57, 135–6
  in al-Ahsa 22, 27, 85
  and Al Sa'ud 14–15, 35–7, 39, 41, 46, 73–6, 78, 89

Ibn ʿAbd al-Wahhab, Muhammad (*cont.*):
  attitudes towards 1
  in Basra 22, 24–5, 27, 49, 57, 85
  and Christian powers 115
  and clerics 37–8, 47–8, 56, 73–6, 80, 128
  death 44
  in al-Dirʿiyya (town) 33, 35–7, 66–7, 70, 92, 101
  fatwas 30–1, 80, 83–4
  in Huraymila 28–30, 49, 57–8, 101
  as *imam* 102
  influences on 22–4
  as interventionist 57, 95, 99–100
  later career 41–4
  legacy 135–8
  as *mujtahid* 56
  opponents 8–9, 27–8, 30–3, 38–9, 47–8, 51–3, 74–5, 77, 80–1, 83–4
  and Ottoman empire 112–14, 115
  pact with Al Saʿud 35–7
  personality 44–6
  private life 44
  regional travel 22–6, 27
  as religious reformer 14, 138
  as self-taught 47, 48–9, 127
  small-town origins 19–22, 47
  in al-ʿUyayna (town) 30–3, 39, 45, 57–8, 92, 93, 101
  writings 15, 45, 48–51, 53–4, 74–5, 110
    Kashf al-Shubuhat 50
    Kitab al-Kabaʾir 50
    Kitab al-Tawhid 29, 49–50
  see also godliness; regime; politics; *tawhid*; Wahhabism
Ibn ʿAfaliq, Muhammad (d. 1750) 32–3, 75
Ibn al-ʿArabi, Muhyi al-Din (d. 1240) 84, 85
Ibn Bishr, ʿUthman (d. 1873) 15, 16, 35–7, 40–1, 70, 78, 102, 111
Ibn al-Farid (d. 1235) 84
Ibn Ghannam, Husayn (d. 1811) 15, 16, 21, 32, 36, 40, 50, 51, 53, 80, 102, 104–5
Ibn Hanbal, Ahmad 20, 32, 38, 53
Ibn al-Qayyim (d. 1350) 23, 50, 51, 84
Ibn Qudama al-Maqdisi (d. 1223) 51, 54, 84, 104
Ibn Rashid of Hail 81, 120, 121

Ibn Saʿud (ʿAbd al-ʿAziz ibn ʿAbd al-Rahman Al Saʿud; d. 1953) 9, 82, 120–1, 122–3, 125
Ibn Taymiyya, Taqi al-Din Ahmad (d. 1328) 23, 50, 51, 66, 84, 87, 93, 137
  Public administration under the shariʿa 100–1
Ibrahim Pasha (d. 1848) 69, 111
idolatry:
  and bedouin 78, 79
  opposition to 27, 28–9, 38, 62, 64, 84, 126
ignorance 21, 27, 36, 55, 77, 126
  and justice 104
ijtihad (independent judgment) 47, 54, 56
Ikhwan 122–3, 129
imamate 89, 102–3, 119
imams 32, 53, 93
  Saudi 36, 102–3
immanentism 83
innovation, opposition to 27, 81, 83, 97
intercession and intercessors 29, 31, 55, 83
interventionism 57, 95, 99–100
Iran (Persia):
  opposition to Wahhabism 9
  and Ottoman empire 25
  and Shiʿism 25–6, 88, 127
Iraq:
  and Shiʿism 26
  US invasion (2003) 132
  see also Basra; Karbala
ʿIsa ibn ʿAbd al-Rahman ibn Mutlaq (d. 1784) 75
Islam:
  pillars of faith 55–6, 62, 87
  and reform movements 23, 37, 111, 121
  as religion of the settled 78
Islamism, political 11
Ismaʿilis, Najrani 43, 46

al-Jabarti, ʿAbd al-Rahman 110
Jaʿfari school of law 25, 26
Jews, as People of the Book 115
jihad 69–71, 126
  against hypocrites 60
  against Wahhabis 116
  defensive 39, 70–1
  offensive 40, 41, 64, 70–1, 101, 123
  suspension 129

jihadism 131–3, 136
jizya (head tax) 115
al-Jubayla, tomb 32, 57–8
Juhany, U. 90–1
Juhayman al-'Utaybi 129–30
jurisprudence (*fiqh*) 20–2, 50, 53–4, 56, 70–1, 104
justice:
  administration 100, 103–4
  social 104–5, 128, 137

Karbala, Saudi conquest (1802) 82, 87, 108
Kharijites 51–2, 93, 96
kufr see unbelief

law:
  customary 77, 78–9, 81, 123–4
  schools of law 20, 52–4, 56, 98, 102
  shari'a 20, 77
literalism, Qur'anic 51, 53
loyalty:
  as fundamental 58–9, 60, 63
  political 14, 25, 37, 40
  tribal 37, 76, 78, 80–1

mahdism 128–9
Mahmud II (Ottoman sultan; r. 1808–39) 112
Maliki school of law 75, 109
Mecca:
  Egyptian conquest 111
  and *hajj* 21, 22, 109
  occupation of Great Mosque 128–9
  *sharif*s 8, 19, 24, 31, 37, 39, 43, 75, 87, 115
  see also Holy Cities
mediation, spiritual, rejection 12–13, 29, 31, 47–8, 55, 83, 136
Medina:
  Islamic University 125, 129
  see also Holy Cities
Midhat Pasha 119–20
modernization, and Westernization 6–7, 13
monarchy, rejection 126, 129
Mubarak (the Great) of Kuwait (d. 1915) 120
*mufti*s 20–1, 31, 53, 101, 103, 124
Muhammad 'Ali (d. 1849) 109–10, 111–12, 117, 119

Muhammad ibn 'Abd Allah al-Qahtani 128–9
Muhammad ibn 'Afaliq (d. 1750) 32–3, 75
Muhammad ibn Fayruz (d. 1801/2) 75
Muhammad ibn Ibrahim Al al-Shaykh (d. 1969) 124
Muhammad ibn Sa'ud (d. 1765) 30, 32, 35–6, 41–2, 43, 46, 88, 99, 101, 102
Muhammad ibn Sulayman al-Kurdi (d. 1780) 75
mujtahid 56
Muslim Brotherhood 6, 126, 129, 132
Muslim World League 125, 132
muwahhidun (practitioners of *tawhid*) 2, 50, 55–6
mysticism, Sufi 24, 28, 31, 85

Nader Shah (d. 1747) 25–6, 87
Najd:
  and Egypt 111–12, 117–18
  and historical sources 15–16
  and Ibn 'Abd al-Wahhab 19–22, 27, 35, 76–7
  and ignorance 21, 77
  and Ottoman empire 19, 27, 108, 110, 112, 114, 119
  and rise of Wahhabism 7, 8, 14, 90–106
  see also First Saudi State; Second Saudi State
Napoleon Bonaparte, invasion of Egypt 5–6, 7, 115–16
Naqshbandi order 24, 28, 86
Nasserism 124, 125–6
nationalism, secular 6, 13, 125–6, 127

obedience, political 42, 69, 97, 98–100, 105, 106, 128, 137
Oneness of God *see* tawhid
oppression *see* tyranny
orthodoxy, and Wahhabism 9–10, 11–12, 51–4, 86
Ottoman empire:
  and Arabia 7
  and Britain 120–1
  and control of Holy Cities 5, 7–8, 24, 108–9, 112
  and First Saudi State 9, 105–9, 111–12, 114–17

Ottoman empire (*cont.*):
  and French invasion of Egypt 5–6, 115–16
  and Ibn 'Abd al-Wahhab 3, 112–14
  and Najd 19, 27, 108, 110, 112, 114, 119
  and Naqshbandiyya 86
  and Persia 25
  and Second Saudi State 119–20
  and Shi'ism 25–6
  and Wahhabism 7–9, 37, 40, 112–14, 115, 119

paganism 21, 31
particularism, political 14, 126, 136
People of the Book *see* Christianity; Jews
persecution of Wahhabis 38–9
Persia *see* Iran
Phillips, Wendell 46
pilgrimage (*hajj*) 21, 39, 109, 114, 121
pillars of Islam 55–6, 62, 87
pluralism, Islamic 9, 12, 24, 47–8, 52, 61, 75, 127, 136
politics:
  and clerics 100–2, 118–19, 123–5
  and commanding right and forbidding wrong 93–4, 94-6, 100, 104, 129
  and Islamic government 96–8, 100–2, 103, 106, 126, 137
  and Islamism 11
  and Naqshbandiyya 86
  and obedience to rulers 42, 69, 97, 98–100, 105, 106, 128, 137
  and pragmatism 45–6, 88, 107, 137
  rejection of monarchy 126, 129
  and tyranny 38, 63, 97, 104–5
  see also quietism; Wahhabism, and politics
polytheism (*shirk*) 26, 29, 36, 51, 55–6, 61, 73–88
  action against 57, 65–6
  and Christianity 115
  and Shi'a 84, 87
pragmatism:
  political 45–6, 88, 107, 137
  religious 75, 106
prayers, communal 31, 94, 98, 108
punishment, Islamic 31–2, 93

Qadiri Sufi order 28, 84, 85
al-Qa'ida 1, 10, 52, 132–3, 136

al-Qasim 76, 110, 114, 118, 120, 122
Qatar, as Wahhabi 10
Qawasim clan 116
quietism:
  and Hanbali school 20
  in Najd 22, 28, 97, 127, 130
Qur'an:
  individual study 47–8, 49, 56–7, 63–4, 127
  and literalism 51, 53

radicalism, religious 126, 127–33, 137
Rafidites, Shi'a as 84, 87
Rashid Rida, Sayyid Muhammad (d. 1935) 121
religion, popular 13, 23, 28–9, 31, 32, 35, 38, 85, 104, 105, 123
remembrance (*dhikr*) 83
rituals, popular 13, 35, 111
Riyadh:
  and al-Dir'iyya 40–1
  Saudi capture 43, 120
  and Second Saudi State 117
  and Sufism 85
Ruthven, M. 10

saints:
  as intermediaries 83
  shrines 24, 32, 57–8, 85–6, 108, 111, 121
Salafism 2, 10–12, 48, 121, 125–6, 129, 133, 136–7
  and Shi'ism 88
Sa'ud ibn 'Abd al-'Aziz (d. 1814) 42, 102–3, 108, 112, 116
Sa'ud ibn 'Abd al-'Aziz Al Sa'ud, King (d. 1969) 125
Sa'ud ibn Faysal (d. 1875) 119
Saudi Arabia, Kingdom:
  and clerics 124–6
  historiography 16
  and jihadism 131–3, 136
  oil revenues 121, 125, 128, 130
  and Ottoman empire 120–1
  and regime of godliness 121, 136, 137
  and religious radicalism 126, 127–33
  restoration 120–1
  as Wahhabi 10, 14
  see also First Saudi State; Najd; Second Saudi State

Sayyid Qutb (d. 1966) 126, 127, 132
Second Saudi State (1818–91):
   and civil war 119, 130
   defeat 119–20
   and Ottoman empire 119–20
   reassertion of power 117–19
   and regime of godliness 118–19
sectarianism, accusations 9, 51–2, 60
September 11 attacks 10–11, 132
Shafi'i school of law 24, 31, 75
Shah Wali Allah (d. 1762) 23
shahada 55, 62, 79–80
Shammar tribal confederation 120
shari'a:
   and customary law 78–9, 81, 123–4
   enforcement 31–2, 36, 77, 103, 113, 126
   and schools of law 20, 77, 78
al-Shawkani, Muhammad 5
Shi'a 24, 27, 63, 80, 86–8
   attitudes towards Ibn 'Abd al-Wahhab 1
   and Bani Khalid 81
   in Basra 25–6, 87
   demands for forced conversion 123
   militant 127
shrines of saints 24, 32, 57–8, 83, 85–6, 108, 111, 121
al-Sindhi, Muhammad Hayat (d. 1751/2) 23, 24
state (*dawla*), formation 89–90, 103, 106
Sufism 24, 31, 51, 53, 83, 109–10
   and Al Sa'ud 86, 108
   and Hanbali school 28, 84, 86
   Naqshbandi order 24, 28, 86
   Qadiri order 28, 84, 85
Sulayman ibn 'Abd al-Wahhab (brother of Ibn 'Abd al-Wahhab) 28, 30, 42, 43, 64, 75–6
Sulayman ibn 'Abd Allah 68–9
Sulayman ibn 'Ali (d. 1668/9) 20
Sulayman ibn Suhaym (d. 1767) 38, 75
Sunna:
   and Ibn Hanbal 53
   individual study 47–8, 49, 56–7, 127
Sunni Islam:
   radical 127
   and Shi'ism 25–6
   and *tawhid* 56, 136
   and Wahhabism 9–10, 51–3, 73–6, 119, 121, 135

superstition, condemnation 32, 38, 79, 83–5, 103

Taif, Saudi sack (1803) 82, 108
Taj (holy man) 38, 84
takfir see excommunication
tawhid (Oneness of God) 29, 36, 48, 49–50, 54–7, 74, 127, 135
   in action 57–8, 94
   al-hakimiyya 130
   al-rububiyya 29, 55
   al-uluhiyya 29, 55
   and politics 83, 97–8, 103
   and polytheists 58–9, 75, 93–4, 115
   and Shi'a 87
   see also excommunication; *jihad*
tax:
   head tax 115
   Islamic (*zakat*) 31, 76, 82, 101, 118
   non-Islamic 36, 37
terrorism, 9/11 attacks 10–11, 132
theology, speculative 51
tombs *see* shrines
transcendence 83
tribes:
   and customary law 77, 78–9, 81
   nomadic 21, 60, 76–8, 80–2
   and Saudi state 82, 122–3
   tribal loyalties 37, 76, 78
Turki bin 'Abd Allah (d. 1834) 117, 118
tyranny 38, 63, 97, 99, 104–5

'Ujman tribe 43
unbelief (*kufr*) 61, 63–4
United States:
   and pressure on Riyadh 129
   terrorist attacks on 10–11, 132
universalism, religious 13–15, 126, 136
'Uthman ibn Mu'ammar 30, 31–3, 38, 39, 41–2, 98–9
al-'Uyayna (town):
   as birthplace of Ibn 'Abd al-Wahhab 20
   and early Wahhabis 39, 41–2
   Ibn 'Abd al-Wahhab in 30–3, 39, 45, 57–8, 92, 93, 101

Wahhabism 5–16
   as anti-colonial 115–17
   as anti-intellectual 49

Wahhabism (*cont.*):
  as desert movement 77, 82
  dissident 128–9, 130–3, 137
  and egalitarianism 60
  and European states 114–15, 119–20
  as exceptionalist 52, 56, 119
  as exclusivist 9–10, 12, 23, 31, 52, 73, 110, 119, 122
  historical sources 15–16, 22
  impact 135–8
  later doctrinal modifications 64–5
  and mahdism 128–9
  opposition to:
    early 32, 37, 49, 74–5, 80
    and First Saudi State 37, 110, 115–16
    and Saudi Kingdom 121, 122, 132
  origins 8–9, 21–2, 37, 89–106
  and orthodoxy 9–10, 11–12, 51–4, 86
  and Ottoman empire 7–9, 37, 40, 112–14, 115, 119
  persecution 38–9
  and politics 1–2, 6–7, 13–14, 37–8, 41–4, 73–4
    and clerics 100–2, 118–19, 126, 130–3
  and Saudi expansionism 108–10, 117, 135
  and state formation 89–90, 103, 106
  and proselytization 109–10, 118–19, 128
  and radicalism 126, 127–33
  and reform movements 23, 37, 111, 121, 130–1
  and Saudi Kingdom 128–9
  as sectarian 9, 51–2, 60
  and Sunni Islam 9–10, 51–3, 73–6, 119, 121
  as xenophobic 117
Westernization, and modernization 6–7, 13
women, right of inheritance 79
World Assembly of Muslim Youth 125
World Trade Center, 9/11 attacks 10–11, 132

al-Zafir tribe 43, 46, 79
zakat (tax) 31, 76, 82, 101, 118
Zayd ibn al-Khattab 32
al-Zubara (town) 76, 110
al-Zubayr (town) 76, 110, 122